THE ONLY ONE SHRIKRISHNA

RAJENDRA CHANDORKAR

Made with ♥ on the Notion Press Platform
www.notionpress.com

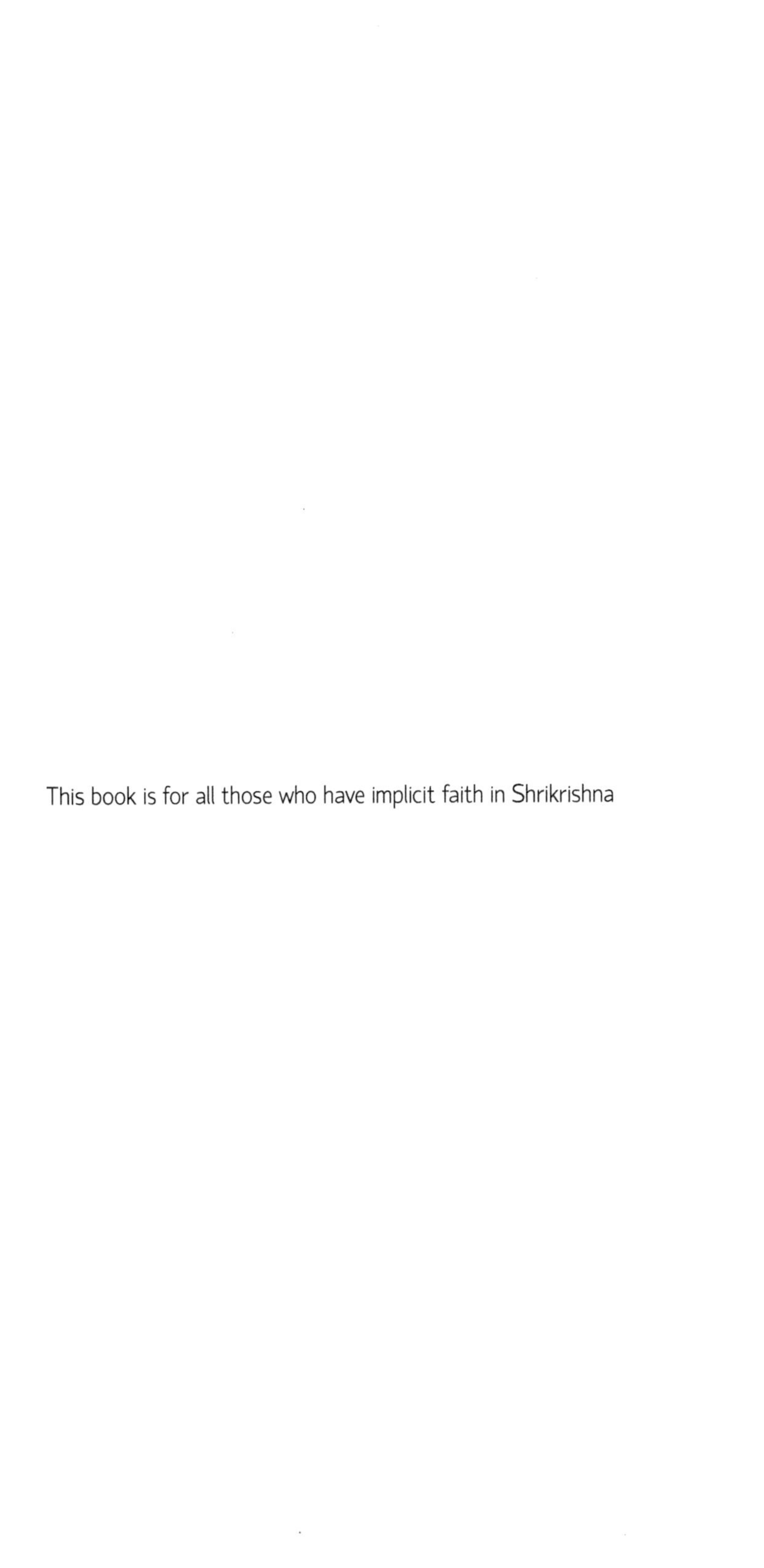

This book is for all those who have implicit faith in Shrikrishna

Contents

Foreword

When my friend asked me whether I would be writing a book on Shrikrishna and that too concerning the current situation in our nation I was not sure. The first thought that struck me was "Does He want me to?" If He does then, writing a small book on him would be easy. It did not, then, matter whether I have the capability or not. He Wants, then, it would happen.

In our school days, we had a poem written by the great pioneer Marathi saint Dnyaneshwar. Our teacher was a devout Vaishnav, and he became just ecstatic when he was explaining what the saint was saying. Dnyaneshwar was seeking permission from the Ved Vyas for attempting to translate his Geeta. He was offering the justification for attempting to write and translate the Geeta in the vernacular Marathi. He gave an example of a swan, the *rajhansa*, which is the most graceful bird with an even more graceful walk. He says that maybe the swan is the most graceful but does that mean that a person like me should not attempt to walk? Then he talks of the sun and a small earthen lamp. We know that the sun is the life giver and probably the brightest, but does it mean that a small lamp should not spread a little light of its own? He also says that when the sun is not around, the lamp gives us the light which helps us fight the darkness. Drawing inspiration from these and having full faith in His blessings, I wrote the first letter, and then it was as if I was under the control of someone who wanted me to write.

I very humbly say that I have written is, whatever, he could get out of me, he would have done a great job himself, but he never does anything himself, he only facilitates his devotees to do something. All shortfalls are due to my limited understanding of his instructions. Like the great Arjun who despite being in front of the Virat Vishwa Swaroopa and with the Divya-Drishti could see only that much which Shrikrishna wanted him to see. I could write, based on what I could pick up from his dictates.

I have *not yet fully* understood Shrikrishna, and I know that I would *never* do so in my lifetime. He is so vast like an ocean, complex like a cryptic puzzle, and at the same time as easy as talking to a friend. From my childhood to every day till today, I feel that Shrikrishna is around me telling and guiding me. Yet due to my limitations, I am still the imperfect one with so many mistakes already committed and so many more would be in the future. But I somehow feel his presence around me. He wants me to think, imagine, and do something to improve the lots of Sanatan dharma. So, this is the first little step towards the same. I hope that it starts the brainstorming so urgently needed for all of us.

We all believers in the Sanatan dharma have to come together now, or it would be very late. We are very near to losing our religion, our nation, our identity, and even our existence. We are told that everything at the top of evolution starts the decay and then becomes extinct. But we must know that the Sanatan dharma is timeless and ageless and it was there when nothing was there and when there would be nothing in the universe. But we also have to understand that it would not be automatic. We all would have to work overtime and stretch beyond our normal limits, and then we may emerge as the victors.

The circumstances when Shrikrishna was with some of our ancestors in the Dwapar Yug, then and now are very similar, as discussed in this book. I hope that at least a few would understand the need of the hour and unite in the interest of the Sanatan dharma and themselves. The existence of the great Bharatvarsha depends upon what we do in the next three decades. Others have a phased-out strategy to phase us out of the globe and we are in our slumber, daydreaming about the non-existent or hypothetical *Ganga-Jamuni* tehjib. One initial baby step is all He wants from you and then he would take you through the entire course, till you finally reach your purpose in life and the common goals of the Sanatan dharma.

I believe in the Word of Shrikrishna that *no more original thoughts* would be possible after the Geeta. So, I do not claim any originality. I have drawn heavily from the teachings of the Geeta, Mahabharat, and the Shrimad Bhagwat. I was introduced to the stories of the Puranas by my grandfather, my mother, and the Gyani Swamiji at the Ramakrishna Math in Nagpur. Later on, I was very fortunate to listen to Mavshi Kelkar, Balshastri Hardas, B.M. Purandare, Go Ni Dandekar, and a few of my intellectual friends. I think that Shrikrishna is best explained to you by some serious peer learning. The first readings were from magazines for the kids like *Chandoba (the Marathi version of Chandamama)*, and then the fiction on the Mahabharat, Ramayana, and Bhagwat. Sessions by Vidyavachaspati Shankar Abhyankar, Govind Aaphale Guruji and his son Charudatta, Dr. Shailesh Pangaonkar, Dr. Sumant Tekade, and many others have opened a lot of thought processes. Books by Lokmanya Tilak, C. Rajagopalachari, Dr. S. Radhakrishnan, Swami Prabhupaad, Iravati Karve, Anand Sadhle, Durga Bhagwat, Ranjit Desai, Shivaji Sawant, so many others helped me to get a reasonable idea about Shrikrishna.

Like so many others, I was always pulled by His magnetic charm and have experienced his inexplicable and soothing presence around me. The mere feeling that he is around is more than enough. It gives me reassurance and great strength. When one learns to walk, he usually gets a finger to hold, some soothing voice to encourage and an appreciation for the first step, however shaky it may be, or some consolation if he falls, I feel somewhat similar when He is around. He comes in various forms in the course of life, but He is there. He comes as a mother, father, sister, brother, grandparent, teacher, friend, wife, son, or daughter, and to top it all as a grandson, and thus he completes our lives. *Without him, everything in our lives seems colourless, and out of tune.* He symbolizes the dynamic churning, the *Manthan* of the thoughts. Not for nothing, he is symbolized by the most colourful peacock feather and the flute which provides such soulful music.Let us hope that under his guidance the Sanatan Dharma once again reaches the top of the ladder and teaches everyone how to conquer the world with knowledge, love, and fairness. That is the only possible salvation for all of us.

Rajendra Chandorkar.

CHAPTER ONE

The basic fact is always overlooked.

<u>The basic fact is always overlooked.</u>

We Hindus are here on the planet earth, for about a hundred thousand years or even more. We tend to forget this simple fact, as we have been wrongly trained to believe that the oldest living people on the earth, were someone else, and they were certainly not the Hindus. That was what they all did, (who were the people from other religions) and sadly we Hindus believed that they were right. Many Hindus still believe that the entire progress is due to the western occupation of India.

The so-called civilizations which are said to exist before us would be in no comparison with the overall grandeur of the Sanatan dharma. They could be good but not as comprehensive as our own. We are told that nothing worthwhile *existed* before say five thousand years. The research now negates this assumption. If you notice any excavation sites, they generally reveal a strong connect with Hindu temples, colonies, artifacts, cultural emblems, and many such things which were unheard of in the erstwhile world. The radiocarbon analysis of many ancient artifacts excavated during archaeological activity anywhere in the world *tells* us that we were the oldest and arguably the best. That it does not matter to a believer of Sanatan dharma, because he already knows that He was there when nothing else was there and He would be there when nothing else would be there.

The stories tell us that we knew the astronomical distances, the time of various eclipses, their effects, and even how to reach various stars. We knew the art of teleportation, telekinesis, igniting the fire at will, projectiles, excellence in metallurgy, medical sciences, surgery, crop patterns, breeding animals and seeds and so many such things which were beyond the comprehension of many people during that period. Very safely speaking even people from today's modern world can rarely understand the highly complicated things done in a very simple way by our esteemed ancestors. Just imagine a person picking up a blade of grass, chanting a mantra, and creating a Brahmastra. He does not need a reactor, plutonium or heavy water, or anything costly, but he produces a deadly weapon.

Imagine a metal pole created in India, with unknown alloy contents standing in open, braving all atmospheric extremes and still standing tall for centuries. It poses a challenge to modern science. The temple of Kailash which is created in a single rock that too from top to bottom, the singing columns of the temples in the south, the swinging columns of the temples, the creation of Dwarka in a jiffy, the creation of May-Sabha, the creation of millions of temples, is beyond the normal perspectives of a common man.

The intricate patterns of a Banaras silk sari or an authentic *Paithani* sari is going on for tens of thousands of years, passing the rare technics to the next generations.

The test-tube babies, the surgeries, the medicines for reviving an almost-dead person, the art of massages, the art of panchakarma, and the art of survival in extreme climates together keep us *wondering if is it real.*

We have to understand clearly that art and rich culturecomes to the fore only when the three basic needs are taken care of. Inner peace which is the prime component for creativity to flourish was in abundance in the ancient Hindus. That they were at peace with themselves and with their creator hugely reflects in their creations. The immense patience and perseverance required for working on time-consuming projects like the temples, or the dams came as an after-effect of the satisfied society where a large section could be allowed to pursue their passions in noble arts, literature, and science.

The doubt in your mind is not normal. Please understand that it is a *cultivated* emotion. Most people who do not like to know or accept that Sanatan dharma is way ahead of their versions of leading lives have deliberately highlighted the so-called shortfalls of our religion without even trying to know what it is like a Hindu. The very sophisticated and suave people accepted themselves as the only ones who know what is to be known about all of us as a creed and were puzzled about the simple fact of how *the sugar juice entered the delicious jalebi.* The fact that Indians were divided and their divisions were encouraged and exploited and later cultured by the invaders for their benefit.

Sanatan religion commonly known as Hinduism is not a religion. Our religion is Vedic. Sadly, many of us are unaware of this simple fact. The origin of the word Hindu is also a hotchpotch. There are many references to the word Hindu in the shlokas much before the advent of Christianity. The Sindhu Hindu is not correct. There is a definition of Bharat, which tells us that it is the land between the mountain and the ocean.

We have to review each and everything that is forcibly embossed on our minds by other men than Hindus so that we would once again be happy and proud to be a part of the Sanatan dharma. We need to study our epics with a newfound zeal, understand them and then disseminate the knowledge in a correct way to the doubting Thomas in our fraternity.

To put things in a proper perspective we have to set time scales at three different levels. Indian history can be viewed in three segments. Each segment is very significant and tells us a lot that has been hidden from an average Hindu.

1. The ancient Vedic civilization
2. The time between 0000 AD to 700 A.D.
3. After the advent of Islam in 700 A.D. to the present day

***

1. The ancient Vedic Civilization: Most modern Hindus are not very well informed, about their roots. There are many reasons but the main reason which stands out is the lack of interest. The fact that we were very superior to all present-day superpowers is very embarrassing for many of them and even for some of the pseudo-intellectuals in India. So, there was a concerted effort to deny the Hindus their rightful place in history. The positions of strengths were changing and even today they are changing. We have recently seen a shift in power on the global scene. The ancient Indians were too far ahead of their counterparts and they were unconscious of that fact. They expected each of the humans to be like them and that is where they *made* their first mistake. They were liberals, they seemingly welcomed the arguments (termed as Vaad -Vivid.). They had a clear idea of why and how they *were*, and where they should be. They had no riddles in their mind, they knew who makes, controls, and destroys the universe. They were scientific, progressive, and law-abiding and they had their rulebooks which even today stand out as the exceptionally written down.

2. From 0000 to 700 A.D.: During this time, it is seen that Bharatvarsha was at the peak of civilization. They were very rich, very cultured, very contented, at peace with the world, and in harmony with nature, they had time to write books and unique epics, construct temples, experiment with science, and lead a full life. The only thing they missed to note was the low levels of the rest of the world, which was to hit them very hard shortly. They expected the rest of the humans as enlightened as themselves, a grave mistake and they paid very heavily and for a huge period.

3. From 700 A.D. to the present day: When the first ship carrying the hapless refugees reached the shores of the Bharatvarsha they were received as per the dharma of the Sanatan people. They treated them like the *Atithi, the welcome guests.* They all soon

became the most unwelcome ones and ousted the house owner. But this act of grace proved to be one of their most stupid acts. That was a bad omen. It created a passage as well as a practice for the people of that part of the world to come to Bharatvarsha and loot.

There was a clash between a flourishing civilization and a deprived barbaric one. The deprivation in the neighboring countries of the invaders made them suspicious and cruel. They were driven by the madness for the money, looting, and forced conversions and they must have been surprised that there was very little resistance. The difference between being a *simple* person and a *simpleton* was never understood by the noble Hindus. *They still cannot do the same.* Their simplicity caused them great distress, a long period of invasions, foreign rule, and slavery. Their prosperity was lost. Their culture was lost. They were divided. They were exploited. They were almost made extinct, and yet they are the ones who are blamed for the communal *hatred crimes* in India. No other community has been exposed to such a continued prolonged, blatantly wrong, and poisonous attack on its culture, beliefs, traditions, and lifestyles. That too by those who were nowhere near the lowest form of Hinduism.

Probably the biggest mistake the Hindus committed was to expect other people as noble as they were. They thought that being noble was a way of life. They did not have an idea of the raw, barbaric, subhuman, and cruel ways of the invaders from the middle east. They are still paying a heavy cost for their ignorance.

***

Ever since the advent of Buddhism religious conversions started. Religious conversions were unheard of in Bharat. All new and emerging religions were supported by the kings and hence conversions were almost protected by the law. The Hindus were the softest target. Some used soft methods to propagate but most of them used the most barbaric methods. The choice was simple either to get converted or to perish. By the way, we must proudly know that Hindus *have never forcibly converted* a single person known. We have been forced to convert brutally by Christians, Muslims, Buddhists, and now communists. No religion is as vulnerable as our own. One reason is we have no *binding force,* present in other religions. No fear of social boycotts or death penalties for simple acts taken as blasphemy. We believe in providing freedom to each of us, real free will. We have so many variations, that we are easy to convert. Independence creates a basic division that is exploited by others. We have no laid down process of worship, as in other religions. We have many books as against the single book versions. We have so many gods as against the one prophet concept. We have to understand that there is a difference between a prophet and God. *No prophet is a God.* That Sanatan dharma has a single controlling power that creates, protects, and destroys is lost on many Hindus.

Over time, many people in our community strongly differed, and they made a lot of noise. Very vocal were people like Charvak, or Kanad. But they were countered intellectually. There was a *vad* and *vivad.* They were never beheaded for their differences. The tradition of *shastartha,* arguments based on logic and sciences was an accepted way of settling a debate. The classical example is the epic debate between Adi Shankaracharya and Mandanmishra. We were mature enough to accept and absorb dissents. So, when these days communists blame us and say that we are unreasonable and intolerant is a matter of serious laugh. Coming from the followers of mass massacres and perpetrators of inhuman atrocities it is unacceptable.

Where the Yogeshwar Krishna says that he can be worshipped with a leaf, or even simple water there should be no confusion. And even if there is an elaborate process of performing puja it is again as per the wishes of the Yogeshwar. He is the one who decides and he is the one who chooses you or someone else to be the man of the hour.

What should be done?

We have to study all other religions and find out the basic nature of how and why they do what they do. Why do they feel the need to increase their numbers by forceful conversions? They use so many ways to allure unsuspecting, ignorant people around the world. The basic and most vociferous argument they use against the Hindu or Sanatan way of life is that there are so many casts, creeds, and factions in Sanatan. They claim that they have only one God and that there are no castes in their faith. There is no distinction based on color, caste, or region.

Let us scrutinize this statement.

Let us begin with the Christians. As of today, they have the largest number of followers. They are well-spread and controlled mostly by the Vatican. Nothing wrong with it. They claim that they are one. There is one Christ and one bible. It is a wonderful way to live. If you check up you would be surprised that there are many factions. The churches of Latin Catholics would not enter the Syrian Catholic church. Similarly, the Salvation Army, the Marthoma, Pentecost, Seventh-Day Adventist, Orthodox, Jacobite, and about 146 such different types follow the same religion but in a different way. As a Sanatan, we do not have any reason to object and we do not. What, we must understand and mark is that none of the above factions enters or shares the other church for prayers. And yet they criticize the Sanatan without understanding the philosophy.

When we turn our attention to Islam, they claim to have one God and one book. We find that there are different mosques for the Sunni, Shia, Ahmadiyya, Mujahidin, Sufi, and thirteen types. There are many more. They usually do not enter or allow other people to enter or pray in their mosque. Their fights are bloody and continue for centuries.

The Sanatan religion has so many books and so many versions of one deity. There are many sects, languages, and different ways of worshipping. Somehow all can enter all temples, worship, and offer prayers.

The followers of the Sanatan have to stress this simple fact in the minds of those who criticize with or without purpose and create a feeling of instability.

The stepwise plan can be:

The <u>first</u> and simplest thing we should do is to tell our kids that they belong to some very powerful way of life. Tell them the names of their forefathers. At least seven. Talk about their roots.

Tell them that their ancestors were very brave and clever. They resisted the forcible conversions, preserved the traditions, and never succumbed to the atrocities. Tell them that those who were afraid, or lured by the forceful conversions have no moral right to talk about us. That they had chosen something else, we have accepted them. Despite being in majority, we did not kill them like their people killing so many Hindus, Sikhs, Jains, and Buddhists. We must have a high and righteous position whenever we talk about Hindus. Teach them the basic mantras, and the power of the same. The Om is the earliest original sound and what NASA says about it. The concept of the naad Brahma needs to be explained.

There is no example in history where a particular community has been persecuted for two thousand years and yet it still survives. Not only survives but leads a major role in world affairs. That it suffered cruel persecution was not always because of the outsiders, looters, and offenders from outside. Most of the trouble was due to the stupidity of the persons who could not adjust to the fact that they were in a superior society and at the top of the evolution cycle. The same problem persists. Even today if you have to be known as an intellectual the easiest path is to abuse Hindus, ridicule their culture, promote some stupidity from the western world, and always say what the masters from foreign countries want. There was a report from KGB which stated that they had infiltrated even the PMO.

That we are here and exist as Hindus is a tribute to our forefathers and their resourcefulness and their refusal to conversions.

<u>Secondly</u>, we must stop criticizing our religion. In no other religion, any person can talk so much baseless things against their gods and be alive. If we do not like something, we should simply shut up. The traps set by the pseudo-intellectuals are seen sometimes, but most of the time they are hidden.

We have to investigate every person who speaks against Hindus. Especially people who use Hindu names even when they are not Hindus. People like Pronoy Roy, Arundhati Roy, N. Ram, every stupid person from JNU, or the AMU, and even the persons who were gifted the plum posts by the congress government as a reward. We have to strongly tell these people that the moment, they or their ancestors for whatever reasons preferred other religion than Sanatan Dharma, they lost the right to criticize the way the Hindus think or live. The fact stands out that when criticized in any which way possible, the Sanatan dharma still is the best option for the entire mankind. Feature by feature, we have to categorically weed out the stupid objections these people propagate against our religion which so far has not even responded. We have not retaliated and that is our mistake. One *book* and one *prophet* type religions can be never in the same class of the Sanatan dharma. We seriously have to estimate the life period of such religions and act accordingly. We need not be *aggressive* but we must be *assertive* about our sanity and ultimate understanding of the relationship of us with our Creator in our religion.

Lastly, we do not have to be defensive about anything, and we need not justify or explain anything about the Sanatan Dharma to any stupid person in our country or foreigners. We have to tell them that even to understand the basics of Sanatan Dharma one needs some elementary intelligence, and even after that, the person can decipher the nine dimensions explained in Sanatan's way of living.

***

CHAPTER TWO

Why Shrikrishna?

Why Shrikrishna?

Most of the active life of any common man is spent deliberating what he should do so that the quality of his life improves. When to do it, how many times, and finally checking and rechecking the current state of life. When he needs to take an informed decision, he does not study and spends time in indecision, then in the later stage of his life he rues over the mistakes or even worse blames everyone for his failures. Throughout his active life, he rarely finds time to cater to his philosophical and theosophical urges. He many times is not even aware of them. They say that intelligent people have more doubts than fools, and maybe it is true!

What about you?

Are you held up?

Are you at least aware that you may have options?

Do you see options?

Have you ever weighed the options?

If you have analyzed the available options, would you continue doing what you are doing, or you have decided to change?

Are you facing the famous "*to be or not to be*" dilemma?

It is also a situation where you are at a proverbial crossroads, and you are not able to decide which way is right for you.

What is the right time to quit or to stick around with what you doing for some more time?

Do you trust your colleagues?

Do you have at least, one single person, the one with whom you can genuinely share your issues?

What is the cost of taking a wrong decision?

How much you would be losing in terms of money, material, prestige, esteem, marital harmony, status in the society you move in, and at last your value in your estimates?

If you feel you are in a dilemma for whatever reasons, due to situations outside your control and your life is not what it should have been, *you are not where you are destined to be*, then <u>the only one Shrikrishna</u> can guide you as he did some thousands of years ago to *one* of the ablest persons, but who had *lost the will to perform* due to some doubts. Shrikrishna not only made him stand up again but helped him to win the war with the external and more importantly internal enemies. The chances of winning the war for the Pandavas were 7:11. The opposition was strong, united, immoral, with more valuable resources, more cunning, clever, and prone to cheat, and yet Shrikrishna helped the Pandavas win the war with complete annihilation of the enemy. Shrikrishna never expected any favors from the enemy. He took advantage of each fault of the enemy and won the war. He never actually participated in the war. He was a mere Sarathi, who had vowed that he would not use any shastra or Astra in the war. Yet, he was the only one *responsible* for winning the war. He was probably the first example of a successful nonplaying captain. As a true leader of the highest quality and unwavering clarity of purpose, Shrikrishna has no parallel in human history.

Whatever your profession, whether you are a teacher, student, administrator, manager, artist, poet, writer, decision implementor, decision maker, military person, politician, or you are just a plain *nobody,* the unacknowledged backbone of the democratic process, or a simple man or a woman, you would be surprised to find that Shrikrishna is as near as you or even slightly more capable in your profession. He can talk to you as an expert, discuss with you and provide solutions to your most complex problems. When you start interacting with Shrikrishna about your unresolved issues, the first thing you realize is that you are not his first case. Your ego is shredded to pieces. You felt so sure, that you and your problem were the worst but afterward, you realize that many like you have been provided solutions and are now happy.

When you read Geeta you come to know that it is one of the most straightforward narrations about how to lead your life, what to expect and what not to, and your limitations as a human, you are, just a means, whatever you think you are doing is because he planned it that way, if you were not to be someone else would do it and probably in a much better way. You understand Geeta differently when you read it the first time and then every time you read it again. When you feel you have got a grip on it some new shade emerges, and you are once more attracted with new vigor.

***

So, from today, whenever you feel you do not have a chance, do not give up, follow what Shrikrishna tells you in the Geeta, understand, apply the knowledge to your situations, and maybe after some time you would be celebrating an unlikely victory. There is a common objection that people throw at your face every time the issue of reading the Geeta arises. They say that they do not understand it. A great story from the life of Adi Shankaracharya can explain things in a better way.

The story goes like this: Once Shankaracharya was visiting a small town and he was with his disciples. He heard very wrong reciting of the Geeta in a loud voice. He approached the person and asked him for the reasons. The meek person was speechless. He was in shock when he saw the sage. But he accepted that he does not know anything about Geeta, or the correct shlokas. He is reciting as he knows, only because he knows for sure, that his Shrikrishna would correct it. Same to same as he had said to Arjun. He was happy in doing so and if Shrikrishna wanted so, he could correct it before listening. So, the matter is about doing things in a way you can, you can later improve. A futile quest of becoming perfect before starting is as useless as not doing anything. He was doing what he was able to and he was sure that his Shrikrishna was understanding what he was doing. Can you be so simple?

In one more story of the same sage, he talks about the futility of learning a language or grammar, etc. It goes like this: In Kashi, the Adi Shankaracharya saw a very old man trying very hard to learn Sanskrit along with grammar. The acharya was very disturbed to see the wrong priority of the person. In an age when he should simply pray, and be devoted to the Sarveshwar, the old man was trying to learn a language that would be insufficient to save his soul. This act of the old man prompted the creation of one of the most beautiful, but hard-hitting poetry called Bhajgovindam.

The central core of the Indian philosophy revolves around the Vedas, Upanishads, and Puranas and the teachings of Yogeshwar Shrikrishna. Any Indian whether a Hindu or not is certainly aware of the significance of Shrikrishna. Whether he has the correct information and/ or impression is a matter of real concern.

Shrikrishna is alive even today in the minds of the Vaishnavas and the minds of other Hindus. But it seems many have not found the correct way to follow him. They are happy in rituals that are of no significance, and no lessons are extracted from these. Whether it is the *Dahi-handi,* the Gokulashtmi, or the Garba dance it does not help their cause. The perverse versions of such activities need scrutiny.

Shrikrishna had so many facets, aspects, and perspectives to his life that one needs a lifetime to know even one. What he was or what he was not, what he stood for, what he planned and what he delivered, are a few things that we should learn. We should learn, to plan, execute, and eventually win, from him.In the entire known and unknown history of mankind, the character of Shrikrishna rules simply supreme. No other known religion has anyone who can be compared with even one aspect of the life of Shrikrishna. The modern history imposed upon the gullible Indians, by the vested interests, the invaders, the leftists, and the different sects, has created unnecessary confusion about this magnificent character. The stupid and almost pediatric arguments have tried to divert the attention from the real core of the Purnavtar, called Shrikrishna. In his entire life, Shrikrishna was always correct, circumspect, concise, and to the point. Add to this his ever-present wit, and we know what a pleasure it must have been to listen to him. He knew his strengths; he was fully aware of the weaknesses of his enemies and hence he could always be on the winning side. He was a conversationalist beyond compare.

Parashar Rishi, the father of the Maharshi Ved Vyas has defined the six essentials for anybody being called Bhagwan. They are strength, fame, wealth, knowledge, beauty, and renunciation. Shrikrishna had all of these and many more. He was in everything and at the same time unattached. He could be very rational about everything around him. He gives information in detail about his richness, in the tenth chapter of the Geeta, under the name Vibhutiyog. Once you start getting closer to the aura of the great Shrikrishna you understand that you as a Hindu are blessed to be one of his *ansha*. When you further read his texts and the Shrimad Bhagwat, you come to know that the purpose of your life is to travel back to the purnaroop of Shrikrishna. Whatever you do between these two events is called Maya. Just like the water, which exists in the forms of droplets, snowflakes, glaciers, rivers, lakes, and even wells would ultimately go to the final destination of the ocean. The journey of each form is *different,* but the *destination is the same.* Again, depending upon their karmas, the humans would either again enter the cycle of "birth and death" or they would reach the final destination of the Vaikunthalok.

Why such a magnificent character is derided as a thief, womanizer, and even a coward is a matter of great concern. It is possible that the original text of the Bhagwat or other epics was changed as per the convenience of the later rulers like Ashok, the Turks, the Mughals, and finally the British. Why everything that is Indian, Hindu, and Vedic has been put to derision in wrong secular India? **It is sick.** Moreover, if it was to be replaced with something worthwhile, we would have understood, but it is not so. Nothing else in the world comes anywhere near to what we have in the Sanatan dharma. What must have been a matter of pride has been reduced to a matter of *perceived shame*. The effort to denigrate Sanatan dharma was organized under the complete protection of the rulers in the Islamic occupation, and later the British rule. What is most saddening, is that even after the Independence the trend continued. **Sadly, with even more *venom*!** The rewriting of history in the manner of "His–Story" to suit the whims and fancies of the secular and pro-Muslim rule of Nehru, was so grossly misleading that most of us were fed upon the false history. The glorification of slavery and the so-called nobility of the Muslim and British rulers was at the highest farcical levels. The communists without any regard for Indian history and culture were given the responsibility of the purposeful derision of Indian culture. The ridicule of the Hindus was almost of a gazetted status. **More the derision, more the awards!** In no other country, nowhere in the entire history of mankind, the majority population of any nation has been put to such a shameful existence. The worst part is that the offenders were and are their own elected people, not the invaders. The concerted and concentrated attack on the Hindus and their philosophy was so intense that Hindus were reduced to being apprehensive and defensive in their own country. It took almost six decades for the rational Hindus to realize the evil designs of the people in power. It took the Hindus sixty years after 1947, to note that their history from 0001 AD to 1000 AD, had just vanished from the records and academics. If the Sanatan dharma was so fragile it would have been abolished by now. One of my teachers used to say that even to understand Hinduism, one *needs* a basic level of intelligence. He further said that all the present-day objections were already existing in ancient India, and many people many times have already answered. There is nothing new and hence it must be ignored or in the worst case tackled in a befitting manner. Why Hindus accept any trash from people from other religions is a question that needs to be seriously answered. Those who never knew anything about Hindus talk more out of compulsion and those who were earlier Hindus, then subsequently got converted to other religions have not been able to stop criticizing Hindu ways of life. What matters and what they must understand is that they **no longer belong** to Hinduism and they should be leading their own chosen life comfortably. They are now *enlightened*; (aren't they?) they *are* with the way of life of their own choice and hence even if Hindus go down the drain, they should not be bothered. They were not satisfied with, what was on offer, hence they changed. But they must do a review of their mental, moral and social conditions after the change.

The history of religious conversion in India since the advent of Buddhism is very depressing. Conversion to Buddhism was less dangerous as it was intra-racial. Further, when Islam came to India (begging for help for their survival) after some time they showed their true colors, to the unsuspecting Hindus. They resorted to the conversions which were bloody and cruel. The Christians were clandestinely smart but equally cruel in matters of conversions. The forcible spread of religion was a new concept for the then-Indians. By the time they got hang of the thing, they were in for a big torture. Villages after villages, towns, and even some regions were forced into mass conversions. The tragedy was that the ones who got converted were *equally* ignorant about their earlier Hindu religion and their new religion. The spread of these religions was intensely monitored, and weekly checked either in the mosque or the church. The extent of the numbers is evident if you check up on the nations and their religions in the early part of the last century. In 1900, there were a few Christian countries and even fewer Islamic nations, but now it is somewhere around **one hundred and twenty Christian** countries and about **sixty** Islamic nations. As regards the Hindus, the only Hindu nation of Nepal has also succumbed to communism. Hindus in India lead a pathetic life! Bharat has been compromised to a worse state of affairs concerning religion.

Every Hindu has to defend his way of life very doggedly and strongly or else there would be nothing left of or for him. Hence, we need to know more about the teachings of the great Shrikrishna. Every Hindu has to remember that Shrikrishna had told us that there would be <u>no more incarnations</u> after the Shrikrishna Avatar. The only thing that would help in preserving the Hindu and Hinduism, would be the strength of unity. The speed at which Hinduism is eroded shows that the future of Hindus is bleak. Hindus are still very naïve, they still believe that they would be able to live in a world, where they would be in a minority. All they have to do is to check the conditions of the Hindus in the neighboring nations. Pakistan, Afghanistan, Bangladesh, and many such nations where the percentage of Hindus has been reduced to nothing. And at the same time, the percentage of Muslims in India is continuously on the increase. Hindus have to think why?

Muslims are smart.

We must *appreciate* their *focused effort* to increase their biological number and their influence in our country as well as in the European nations. Hindus also have to understand that no Muslim countries ever allow any Muslim refugees in their Islamic countries. They deliberately help their poor brothers to seek refuge in liberal countries. And then demand their rights. They are on the rise in their number and similarly the count of Islamic nations. *They must be doing something right.* Hindus have to understand that *unity,* if at all possible, between Hindus and Muslims is a temporary and uncomfortable alliance. It is a myth. Their own have never been accepted. So, the question of Hindu-Muslim brotherhood is impossible even if the Hindus accept the same. It would be there only till such a time when the number of Muslims is less than Hindus. The day the Muslims are in majority, Hindus can kiss goodbye to *unity.* There are examples from the history and recent past. Hindus cannot afford to be nearsighted. The entire existence of Hindus depends upon what Hindus do in the coming three decades, beginning in 2020.

Hindus have to understand the defective narrative of the *ganga-jamuni* way of life. The nonexistent way of life! There is nothing of give and take in this. Muslims only take in this type of arrangement. They took Pakistan as their Islamic State. But a greater number of Muslims did not go to Pakistan. They stayed back banking on **the**

proven stupidity of Indian leadership. Now that they are almost thirty percent they would resort to the same tactics and try to break away from India. Muslims, all over the world are playing a *dangerously waiting* game. They are waiting for their numbers to increase, they are waiting while they get all the facilities as the minority, and they are waiting for the right moment when they would start their efforts to strike back and take over the nation in question. **They have not used any weapons, but they have played upon the natural stupidity of the liberals across the globe.** They have successfully done this in fifty-seven nations. The early residents are not at all seen in these nations. They are either converted or they are dead.

The biggest defeat for the Islamic thinkers and their frustrating disappointment is their inability so far to achieve a full conversion of India into an Islamic nation. They are here for almost twelve hundred years; they tried all inhuman methods unsurpassed in cruelty and yet there are about one hundred crores of Hindus remaining. When they came, both Muslims and Christians there were very few in number, but now they are in a sizeable percentage of the population number, even after the creation of Pakistan. Not only that, but they are also somehow more united than the Hindus. They never abuse their religion or their nation. they are united in any issue that involves the defeat of Bharat or Hindus.

Even the new entrants the neo-Buddhists are also on the rise. At whose expense all these religions are growing and proliferating at such a great speed? They probably know, *that if they wait long enough*, they would be successful and they would be more than helped by a stupid section of Hindus, pseudo-liberals, and the planted/ cultivated people in the government. Their machinery is working at a very sedate pace, but they are moving forward. Not only that, but they are more united than the Hindus. At whose expense all these religions are growing and proliferating at such a great speed? The Hindus!

***

What are the Hindus doing?

<u>Nothing much really!</u>

They are still busy with their famous infightings. They blame every available person, but conveniently forget that they are the main culprits for the fall in the faith in Hinduism. They are the main part of the problem which they kept pending for the last two thousand years. The Hindus forget, that they are for all others who are following Christianity or Islam, just worthless Hindus, the *kafirs,* and they must be brought under the patronage of either Allah or the God in heaven. Other than this their existence is meaningless. If the final war happens as it did in Kashmir, Pakistan, Bangladesh, Bengal, Kerala, Nagaland, Goa, and in any such area where their population percentage exceeds that of the Hindus, rest assured that the Hindus would be like the seating ducks and would be either massacred or converted. In another thirty years from 2020, either the Hindus would have to *unite* and *fight brutally* for their existence, or else they would be eliminated. No God or no friends would be able to save you and your race. Presently, the Hindus are thinking like "If I do not eat the tiger, the tiger would also not eat me" very naïve to say so.

If you care to move around the coastal areas in the entire of India, in Kashmir, in all packets where you are in minority, you should see your bleak future. They just do not want you; it is that simple.

If you still do not want to believe and still want to believe in the pseudo-secular shit served to you, you should check up on the following.

- What happened in the Muslim, Christian, and Sikh areas in the recent past?
- Are Hindus safe in their own country?
- What is the source of the cultivated hatred against the rightful residents of the country?
- Why the Aryan vs Dravidian divide was created? Who benefitted from the same?
- Who created language problems?

- What is the percentage increase in the numbers of mosques, churches, buddha-viharas, and gurudwaras?
- How many Hindu temples were destroyed?
- Why only Hindu temples are under the control of the government?
- Why the money collected from Hindu temples is spent on the upkeep of the worship places of other religions in India?
- In no other nation, the majority population is subjected to such bad humiliation as in India.
- How can anyone freely abuse the Hindu religion and culture?
- Freedom of speech is used only against the Hindus.
- Why the minority like Muslims, Christians, and communists allowed to create their strongholds in the form of JNU, AMU, Jadavpur, Vellore, and so many such places? They are openly anti-Indian and anti-Hindu.
- The major part of print media, press, and electronic media are controlled by pseudo-seculars.
- Why education was in the hands of minorities, entertainment in the hands of Muslims, and history in the hands of leftists?
- Why Nehru was preferred over Patel?
- Why Netaji Subhash Chandra Bose was relegated to the backseat?

We have never asked ourselves these questions.

***

One more aspect of Hindus is that they are unnecessarily defensive. They know that they are in the best nation, best religion, and best culture, and yet they are worried about the criticisms from the people who do not matter. Hindus are aware that they are on the brink and that they have to do something, but they do not have a roadmap. **They do not have dedicated leadership.** If someone is there, he does not enjoy the faith of the majority of followers. Hindus have complicated matters regarding their religion and how to follow the same authentically. Hindus in the north have somewhat different perceptions than the Hindus in the South.

Sadly, even after two thousand years of persecution Hindus have not understood the need for *unification*. Once we survive over others, and **when we have no opposition**, we can once again fight for our intra-religious thoughts. The Hindus have forgotten *vayam panchadhikam shatam*. For any offense, from others following other religions like Islam or Christianity, we must be one. Or very soon we would be no more. Sanatan dharma is more talked about by those who have **limited bandwidth of the capacity to understand.** We have to discard most of them and their comments as worthless. Maharshi Aurobindo has said "*We speak often of the Hindu religion, of the Sanatan Dharma, but few of us know what that religion is. Other religions are preponderatingly religions of faith and profession, but the Sanatan Dharma is life itself; it is a thing that has not so much to be believed as lived. This is the Dharma that for the salvation of humanity was cherished in the seclusion of this peninsula from of old. It is to give this religion that India is rising. She does not rise as other countries do, for herself or when she is strong, to trample on the weak. She is rising to shed the eternal light entrusted to her over the world. India has always existed for humanity and not for herself and it is for humanity and not for herself that she must be great.*"

Despite such a wealth of excellence and intellect, we are still looking up to someone alien to explain and endorse our greatness. We feel that unless someone certifies nothing that is Hindu can be good. We forget the fact that we do not need any endorsements not in the least by those who have their axes to grind. None of the foreigners who are acknowledged as the authority on the Vedic religion has separated his religion and set of beliefs when he explained his interpretations. They have conveniently and may be intentionally intermixed the contexts and tried to show that their beliefs are better. Nothing wrong with it. What is hurting the Hindus is the blind following of these people, by the brown sahibs in India. The outsiders can say whatever they want to but when a supposed insider talks about his own it is more disparaging and can have more *impact*.

So, what should the Hindus do? Firstly, they must unite. How does that happen? We have to find a solid unifying factor. The best option available is the teachings of Shrikrishna. What he did in his time we must find out and start using the same. For against anyone who is not Hindu we should be one or very soon we would be a big zero.

Unity on a regional basis, religion, and language, is a must.

1. Maybe, we would have to do a change here or there but the basic plan would not change too much.
2. The internal cleansing of the thought process is a must. Wherein we have to develop a process for the removal of the negative impacts by others and our defective samples.
3. The reassertion of the Sanatan self-esteem is a must.
4. The plan to organize the disoriented Hindu youth. What Swami Vivekanand did is a proven example of the power of Sanatan dharma on the minds of the youth.
5. We must learn to retaliate with logic and correct action on the stupid verbal, and media attacks on Sanatan dharma.
6. We have to seriously work on the process of image management of the Sanatan dharma. We have to wipe out all that stupid nonsense that the western philosophers have spread for purpose of degrading Sanatan dharma.
7. We have to act now or we would be extinct as Hindus.

Shrikrishna also did the same.

The physical cleansing of any race is important but more important is inner cleansing. Shrikrishna did both and he did not only for the people at that time but for the people in the future. The path of truth, and practical smartness is the one that is still guiding us in times of duress. The existence of Hindus is largely due to the correct teachings of Shrikrishna. That is why we are still around and so far, exist. After Shrikrishna, Adi Shankaracharya, Chanakya, Chaitanya Mahaprabhu, and Dnyaneshwar, many extraordinary Ranas from Rajasthan singlehandedly fought the cruel invaders from Mideast and Mongol countries, Samarth Ramdas, Shivaji Maharaj, Dharmaveer Sambhaji, Swami Vivekanand, revived the Sanatan dharma. There must be thousands of others, who must have sacrificed their everything including lives. In recent times Veer Savarkar spent his life in the improvement of the Hindu lots. We can go on naming great souls from across India and even outside. Unless we understand what, we have to do and then actually do it in a concerted and collective manner in a sustained way over a long period, we do not seem to have any future.

The point is simple either we <u>do *it now*</u> or then we may not need *to do anything.*

***

CHAPTER THREE

The Complete Character of Yogeshwar Shrikrishna

<u>The Complete Character of Yogeshwar Shrikrishna</u>

It is highly improbable, if not impossible to sum up the complete character of Shrikrishna. He is the foremost, the *Aadi*, the *Anant*, the *Sakar*, the *Nirakar*, the *Sagun,* and the *Nirgun*. He is larger than anything known and he can create or destroy as per the need. He can be in *sthoolam* or *sooksham* (macro or micro) forms at the same time. There is nothing he cannot do. It is so much complete, so comprehensive, so much encompassing, that one has to expand and extend all his capacities to even understand that he is *not able* to understand the great Shrikrishna.

To put things in a proper perspective let us see the comparison between the two most read and narrated epics of the Bharatvarsha. The Ramayana and the Mahabharata.

The Valmiki Ramayana with all its greatness is about twenty-four thousand verses. Ramayana is translated into almost all languages. In the later centuries, Tulsidas Ji composed his version as Ramcharitmanas. They include the doha, chaupai, and eight such types, as the variations in the composition. They are recited in a specific way and they make it very interesting. The spread of the epic in the Indian subcontinent is dedicated to the Tulsidas' version of Ramayana. Tulsi Ramayana has about 10902 verses. And then there are so many versions that have a huge number of verses. Ramayana represents a specific way of life and many believe that it teaches the proper way of leading life. People try to find solutions in their lives in the epic.

When we turn our attention to the life of Shrikrishna and the narration in the Mahabharata, we are amazed to see the creativity of Maharshi Ved Vyas. Mahabharata is the largest epic which has about (200000) two lakh verses. It includes everything about human life and existence. It also has the Bhagwat Geeta, which means the song of the Bhagwan.

The other accomplishments of the Ved Vyas include the classification and detailing of four Vedas. Before him, the Vedas were in an assorted form. Ved Vyas not only mastered them but also formally divided into the four known forms of them. He also wrote all eighteen Puranas. As if it was not enough, he also authored the entire set of Upanishads, he also wrote the Mahabharata which is the largest single poetic composition in human existence. In addition, he also scripted the Yoga Bhashya and Brahma Sutra. He was so prolific that even in today's computer era, it would be unparalleled. The largest poetry in English is either The Paradise Lost by John Milton. It has ten volumes and about ten thousand verses. The other long poems like The Iliad and the Odyssey combined are ten times smaller than the Mahabharata itself.

We are dealing in detail with the Ved Vyas because we must know that even in times as early as six thousand years, we were very *cultured*, *evolved*, and *rich* in literary traditions.

The prolific writer had no machines to help him. He was in search of a writer who could take down the dictation in the correct way and could maintain the speed of the Vyas. It is said that Shri Ganesh was approached for taking down the text and verses. Ganesh accepted the challenge but with a condition. He told Vyas that he would not wait even for a moment for the next shloka, to which Vyas provided a counter. He asked Shri Ganesh if he would have to understand the first shloka before proceeding to the next. Just for the sake of understanding, think about the duel between the best. It shows that in those days a human being was able to compete with gods. It also shows that in those days only karma mattered, not the birth of a person.

<u>The final punch is yet to come</u>.

After the great war of Mahabharata, Maharshi Vyas was very distressed. He was devoid of any internal peace. He had probably, what we call in the present days, the creative block. He was restless and was trying to reorient his life. He had seen so much worse in human life. He had seen the futility of war, he had seen the destruction of about thousands of humans, horses, elephants, and so much waste of other resources. Maybe, he was holding himself responsible too. In some way, he was the originator of the characters in Mahabharata. He was once again approached by the Devershee Narad. They had a discussion and at the end of it, Narad told Vyas, to write the Shrikrishna-Charitra. So, Vyas simply wrote the Sri Mad Bhagwat. He was getting older and wary, but what he composed in the form of the Bhagwat is in itself very exclusive, it has no known parallel. One man so prolific in creating so many superlative literary creations is simply unheard of.

***

It is very well known that understanding Shrikrishna is very difficult. Does it then mean that one should not try to know him? Not exactly, on the contrary, one should just start with whatever he has by way of knowledge or ignorance, just offer all his self to the great Shrikrishna. If he so desires, he would help the person in his quest. He would try him, test him, and only when Shrikrishna finds the person worthy he is taken to the Vishnu Lok. The moment one can do this he becomes a part of the great existence with Shrikrishna. Shrikrishna has himself made very simple for his Bhaktagan. He said "You can all worship me, love me, and even talk to me if you do it with all your *shraddha. It may be a leaf, an ordinary flower, or a fruit and if you do not have even this you may simply use water.* I would be happy and make you my bhakta". Shrikrishna is simply huge, larger than life, or correctly put in as larger than anything present or imagined or described anywhere in the entire mankind. He knew what he was and more surprisingly he was extremely comfortable with it.

He did not have to act like an actor. He was dark as a cloud but not blue as fondly depicted. He was teased and poked fun at, because of his dark color. You would be surprised to know that he was never formally named in childhood. He was referred to as Kala, later Kanha. He must have suffered a lot. All his names like Shrikrishna, Nandan, Murlidhar, Girdhar, and Madhusudan were added later by people as he went on in his life. He never pretended to be a god, <u>he said hewas.</u> He had no airs to say so. He could mix with the people with ease. So, much so that his childhood friends readily accepted him as one of them. Very ordinary and common! They played with him, they fought with him, and they were never aware of his being the Supreme. His childhood pranks were as common as any other child, he shepherded his cows as any other kid in the Gokul.

There were many attacks on Shrikrishna, by his uncle Kamsa. As Kamsa was warned by the Devershee Narad, Shrikrishna would be his nemesis. Narad also confused Kamsa about how should he count the newborn sons of Devaki. With all his power and pride Kamsa was at the end of his wits and he had started dying long before the eighth was born. He was living in terror and had become paranoid to such an extent that he ordered the killing of all newborns in his state. We know that Shrikrishna had to just finally kill him as a matter of formality. It is a great lesson for *all present-day tinpot leaders,* that a mere threat to life can take the juice out of life. All the money, land, power, friends, and puja path, seem useless when the threat of death looms large.

That Shrikrishna every time found a way to remain alive, is a tribute to his greatness. Whether it was Putana, Kalia snake, or Shakatasur, many other times somehow managed to remain alive and smiling.

Two or three things in the childhood of the great Shrikrishna, are inexplicably hyped. That he was a *Makhan chor* (a thief who is stealing butter) which he was not. It is also told that once when Yashoda finally had enough and asked her mischievous son to open his mouth. What she later saw was beyond her comprehension and she just fainted. She could see the entire universe.

Shrikrishna had a great justification for his eating butter or other things from any household in the Gokul. For him, **everything belonged to him** so there was no question of his stealing anything. He took what was *his* rightfully. But this aspect has been overexposed by the people of other religions. They conveniently and forcefully say that your god is a thief and Hindus stupidly accept.

The second thing which is unnecessarily overhyped is the scene with *Raas Leela*. Shrikrishna was supposed to be in Nandgram when he was about seven to ten years. He must be hardly eight years when he was supposed to have entertained hundreds of *gopis by* partnering in the Raas Leela, a type of erotic dance. Even if this was true it has no real significance. He should be remembered for many better accomplishments. One has to keep in mind that when Shrikrishna left for Mathura, he was just about ten tears. So, it seems that the descriptions of Raas Leela are more of a figment than a real thing. What might have happened is a matter of conjecture! In Vrindavan, even today many believe that the Raas Leela still takes place, and no one enters the sacred and mystical place.

Probably *Raas Leela* appealed to the later generations of poets. It is so full of romance, fantasy, and even ecstasy. It is also what a common man would probably like to do himself. It is very sweet, the mere thought of loving someone with complete abandon is very alluring and especially ladies simply love it. All ladies irrespective of their looks or lack of them could be the most desirable at the same time. The concept of Kanha loving and satisfying every one of the gopis is unbeatable and very charismatic.

Many explanations have been on offer about how and why the Raas Leela was performed. Many people have been involved in vilifying the act without really understanding anything. They have intentionally highlighted this event when it should have been simply ignored. They used it to dilute the magnanimity of Shrikrishna and also the greatness of Hinduism. They ridiculed it and made it one of the most misrepresented events. They shamelessly compared with people like Rasputin and others and belittled the ancient Indian culture. The Hindus who believe in this narration should check up on their grey matter.

But Raas Leela if at all happened, has limited importance in the entire perspective of Shrikrishna's life. It is again a matter of choice of a person what he wants to opt for.

What is more important in the stay of Shrikrishna at the Gokul, Vrindavan, and Nandgram is the way he created a unified force, what he could achieve by way of uplifting their spirits, what he demonstrated to each one of them what could be achieved if they think alike. He demonstrated the logic of strength and staying together. It is known that they were in a terror of the king. They could not even imagine any improvement in their daily routine. They did not know prosperity. Probably Shrikrishna was the first who organized the proper animal husbandry and milk processing etc. He developed methods to encourage progressive farmers.

He used available resources at his disposal, he used a simple bamboo for the creation of a flute. He created magical music out of it. He used simple flowers for his Vaijayantee-mala. He used rags for making a ball. He cleaned the poisonous waters of the river Yamuna. Symbolically, he defeated the Kaaliya snake, but if you look at it rationally, he removed the major pollutants from the river. It is sad that the Yamuna even today is once again polluted and is awaiting one more Shrikrishna-like person.

He demonstrated the importance of the Govardhan mountain, he even asked his people to worship the visible mountain than the invisible far-off god of rains. When Indra retaliated with excessive rains and tornados, Shrikrishna once again underlined what is possible if everyone applied his strength. He asked the people to use their sticks as a support and at the end, he used his little finger to lift the mountain. The single act of his proved to Indra, that he is not as powerful as he thought he was.

Our teacher however told us the inside story, which explains the intricate working of the human mind.

Out there when all Gokul residents were obeying the small kid and praising his powers, some of them, like the present-day leftists in India, started to mock the whole process. They were moderately successful. So, when Shrikrishna saw this, he just removed his little finger for a moment. The mountain started coming down, and the first to flee were the ones who were mocking. The point was proven by Shrikrishna who also *isolated* those who were not on the right side. All of us have to do the same, *identify* and *isolate* all those dirty minds, who are not with the nation. Get rid of them irrespective of their caste, creed, and religion. We have to be extremely vocal about the treachery of such people. **The rule is simple "*nation first!*"**

Shrikrishna was a leader beyond compare. He remained calm every time others were jittery and terrified. If he so desired, he could have done everything he did in his *entire* avatar in a matter of a jiffy and gone back to the Vishnu Lok, but he wanted that we should learn from his life that no problem is without a solution. *No help comes if we do not apply ourselves to solving a problem.* He also taught in a simple way that seeds of solutions are spread around us, and if we look for them, we do find clues.

Shrikrishna was aware of the impending threats on the Sanatan dharma. So, he went out of his usual way and explained what is expected of all of us when things would go wrong. He explained things in a gudh, mystical way, and at the same time, he gave a self-explanatory manual for all of us. He used a strong dose of transactional analysis and situational analysis. He demonstrated his theories in practical ways. He was successful with his available resources.

All his wisdom was forgotten in the subsequent Kaliyuga, and as a result, the Bharatvarsha suffered very heavily. We even lost our ancient name to something alien *as India*. We were convinced by some impractical philosophies and forgot the treasure of our tried and tested wisdom. We surrendered before the people who were and are intellectually *inferior* to us and accepted them as our rulers. We were sure that the invaders would meet their karma and waited for that to happen. We had a very easy way of compromising, *we placed* our lives before that of the nation, land, religion, and culture and accepted conversion to other religions as a safer option. The conversion of the Hindus to Buddhism, Islam, and Christianity is the darkest chapter in the entire existence of our nation, the Bharatvarsha. Sadly, the problem persists today and probably has assumed even more madness against the nation. The readymade justifications, the ever vilifying of Hindu beliefs, the hype of benefits if one gets converted, and the silent support of the erstwhile government in getting the people converted, are the problems that need immediate attention. The reorganization of Hindu beliefs into something more acceptable and *easier to follow routine* is a must or else we are on a fast slide to the end. Whether our religion is great or not is not a matter of discussion, but the fact remains that due to the dark period of Islamic occupation and the subsequent even worse British occupation the Hindu esteem was mauled to such an extent that a new foundation needs to be undertaken. We have to assert that we are the best and must believe in the same. We need to take pride in our knowledge, wisdom, and culture, and most importantly it must be exhibited in our daily routine. Each Hindu is equipped with a better *life toolkit* than any other existing religion and hence it must reflect on his face. Not for nothing Hindu religion has survived the worst persecution, and exploitation, known in the entire history of human existence, and that too for the longest period. We have to understand and propagate that Sanatan Dharam is better than any one-book and one-prophet options. Hindus have to understand that if anything <u>exists in the majority does not mean that it is right</u>. On the contrary, throughout the history of mankind, it is always the people in the intellectual minority who have created benchmarks, and inventions and helped the *thankless* majority. However, in the present days in Bharatvarsha, the minority population concept is twisted, marauded, exploited, and used against (the only place in the world, where at least as of date) the Hindu majority. How long the status would be maintained is up to the unity of Hindus as others have a chalked-out, closely monitored, and funded program to destroy the age-old wisdom present in the Sanatan dharma and drag all mankind to some stupid, impractical *isms*. If Hindus are destroyed the blame would be entirely on the myopic Hindus, pseudo-seculars, and the puppets handled by the outside people with vested interests. You cannot be unhappy unless you allow someone to do so, similarly, no one can destroy you unless you allow him to do so. Hindus have to understand the simple fact, that they are the major targets of Islam and Christians.

The reason for the downfall of Hindus is the fact that Hindus never spread their religion by force. At the same time, they allowed others to land in India, and spread their religions in any which way possible. That most of the world was influenced by the Sanatan dharma long before the advent of other religions is obvious from the excavations all around the world. The temples, the idols, the carvings, and the metal artifacts bear testimony to this. We were very advanced in allowing people to practice Hinduism in the way they wanted. Every dissent was welcome and was accommodated. All the present-day stupid objections to Hinduism were handled with a lot of restraint and respect well thousands of years when the present-day advanced people were wiping their backsides with leaves.

So, we have to seriously think about *where we went wrong*. We must delve into the fact without the proper practice of religion, no civilization can survive. Animals can, but not humans, the reason being the selfishness in humans, and the wicked tendency to store more than needed. We have to think about the strengths of Sanatan dharma which helped it survive the most vicious, inhuman, and long-life attacks by Islam and Christians. We have to devise ways of communicating with those who were converted by force, deception, false promises, and allurements. We have to come out of the engraved and even embedded inferiority complex by the invaders. We have to understand that with all their wisdom they had to come here, loot our resources, exploit us, and still look like they were benevolent. Hindus never needed any such nonsensical violence to *survive*.

We have to identify those who created stupid concepts like excessive non-violence. They hammered the concept of _ahimsa parmo   dharma_by   spreading   half-truths. "अहिंसापरमोधर्म्म:धर्म्महिंसातथैवच:" The complete shloka does not only say this stupid thing, but it also says that the _himsa_ in the purpose of protecting the dharma, is many times better than the ahimsa practiced by the weak.

Ahimsa is a matter of prerogative and not compulsion. If you need to kill you can, but you would refrain unless proven beyond limits. Excessive non-violence is stupid. None of our deities is without a designated _shastra._ The Sudarshan chakra, Gada, dhanushya, khadag, vajra, and to add the _astras_ like _Brahmastra_ tell us that we were never a weak nation, that is why even after trying all _saam, daam, dand, and bhed,_ for nearly two thousand years, the invaders on our land and the religion, are still smarting under their wounds of failures. The dream of "_ghazwa e hind_" is still a distant dream. It is so disgusting to know that these dirty-minded people have plans to such a level that they would either kill or convert the last standing Hindu before which the day of judgment, would not arrive and they would not be judged by their Creator.

It is said that somewhere in the fifteenth century, a pope of the Vatican, took a map of the world, and divided it into two. He gave orders to the famous duo of Columbus and Vasco de Gama to proceed and capture the world in the name of Christianity. As per the story Columbus was supposed to convert America and the Vasco to the oriental world. They nearly succeeded, except in India. They never were anywhere near Islam in matters of cruelty, looting, or cheating, but they were not very far away. They tried all things which helped in the derision of the Sanatan dharma. The forced conversion was a rule in the Portuguese regime in Goa and during the entire Islamic rule in Bharatvarsha.

The problem with India is the excessive number of traitors. Even in ancient times, it was always the traitors who facilitated the cause of the invaders or the enemies of the state. We know so many from so many different times that we do not need to go into the details.

The sad part is that the trend is still going strong in present-day India. After the independence in 1947, we faced a systematic attack on the roots of Sanatan dharma. People with questionable origins and intents have assembled and proceeded to pollute the minds of the younger generations. Traitors are not necessarily present only in the political side of the picture but they are present in the cultural, educational, sports, executive, legislature, and worst in the judiciary. They act like a sleeper cell, they behave in a normal way until such time they are summoned by their masters to belittle, deride and defame the country. With the advent and expansion of digital media, the control over what should be and what should not be shown is a serious mess. Their reach is tremendous, intentions doubtful and loyalty towards India is minimal. They operate through the noble cause of NGOs but very rarely present a nationalist picture. In recent years the new concept of the NOTA option in election voting has been introduced. In the broader sense, they are a breeding ground for traitors.

It all started with the depiction of poverty in India. Movies in stark black and white colours, the darkest backgrounds, won awards from the Western and American world because it suited their propaganda. Why show **only** the dirty side of the picture? Why show India as a snake charmer's country? Why a rickshaw puller, why a labourer in the farms, why the slums in Mumbai and Kolkata, why the upper caste as corrupt, why the Hindus as the faulty side, why the minorities always the fairest, why churches and majars better places than the temples, such questions are not answered even today. There can be many more examples, but even these are sufficient to prove the concerted and concentrated effort against the Sanatan dharma and Hindus. Their system is perfected over some time. How can you otherwise explain a sudden attack on something national and patriotic-spirited occasions? The worst attacks in recent times are on the army, judiciary, election commission, parliament, reserve bank, stock exchanges, and all such places when it is doing something for the nation. Moreover, the people who orchestrate these attacks have *never been elected,* and have a vote share in fractions, but they vociferously attack the functioning of the government and sadly get away with it. They are the loudest voice for the freedom of speech only when it suits them. The moment it is not so they would keep mum and go into hibernation. They are very selective about whom they would support. They are shameless in propagating falsehood. They feel happy when India as a nation is on the losing side. They celebrate when extremists and terrorists kill our army men and poor people. They are the worst infection in the country.

They used a gap in knowledge in the earlier days of independence. They talked of removing poverty but only succeeded in removing the poor. They ruled the state as their fiefdom. In some cases, worse than the British and Islamic invaders. They distorted history, they diluted the valor of Hindu warriors, they defamed people like Shivaji, Sambhaji, Maharana Pratap, Bajirao, Ranjit Singh, Tatya Tope, Rani Laxmibai, Bhagat Singh, Tilak, Subhash Chandra Bose, and Savarkar. A completely false narration was handed over to the primary school students who started believing in the false history. By far this should be the <u>worst crime</u> by the pseudo-seculars against the nation. They have erased about a thousand years of history from the curriculum. They glorified all Muslim rulers who were necessarily cruel and wanted to convert entire India into an Islamic state. All Islamic rulers wanted to establish a caliphate. One can safely say that no Muslim ruler was pro-India. They had scant respect for anything that was Hindu. They killed many saints, Gurus of Sikhs, and common men by the millions. The stories of the mountains of the kafir skulls by each Islamic ruler are present in their documents.

One more falsehood is propagated about the Muslim rulers, that they were very interested in the arts and culture of India. If a study is undertaken even on a surface level the truth would surface. Try to find what in the form of arts existed in Iran, Arabic Countries, Mongolia, and other invading countries during those times and you would know that they were barbaric, devoid of any culture, and very primitive. All the talks of carpets, silk, music, Shayari, and cuisine, fall on the flat face when you trace back their history. One basic thing we have to understand is Muslims just ethnically cleaned country after country like what they did to Iran and the Parsees, Eastern India, the Bengalis, Turkey, and the Turks. It is very much like the modern-day taking over of companies by corporate sharks. When any company is taken over or bought by these sharks, the people who suffer the worst are the existing employees. One day they are suddenly left without any benefits and become the most expendable asset or liability as the case may be. Muslims gave a simple choice to the unsuspecting population of the invaded nation, *"either convert or perish"* so most people accepted Islam rather than death.

When such people once again started working for their livelihood, after their forced conversion, they were with the same skillsets, and hence they did the same things, but under a Muslim name. Like in Benares, a weaver who used to weave a Benasrai silk saree continued doing so, but with his name changed. The brass workers in Uttar Pradesh, the jute workers in Bengal, the cotton growers in Berar and Andhra Pradesh, and the sailors in Western Maharashtra and Gujrat, provided a ready-to-work labour force to the Muslim invaders. The same logic would apply to cuisine, clothes, and all other earlier things. They shamelessly looted even the culture of the country.

But can we really blame them?

The answer would be "no we **cannot**." They were supposed to do what they did, they were instructed by their religion. They were behaving as per the instructions of their religion with full faith. What baffles us is the small number they were in and yet they managed to rule, loot, rape, convert, and spoil the nation. We are more responsible than them. One more thing we have to remember is that those who were freshly converted were even crueler, as they wanted to prove to their new masters their loyalty and commitment. For example, the Bahmani Sultan or the commander Malik of Allaudin Khilji. Apart from a few in the initial years, almost all Muslims in India were converted, though today they try to trace their origins to the deserts of Arabia. Even today the leaders have the same story.

A somewhat similar story can be with the British occupation. Sometime around the Akbar regime, the Britishers came to India as traders. Their main target was the spices and the sea trade. They acted smartly and got permits for warehouses in different parts of the country. When they saw the inherent innocence (read indifference) of the local Indians, they started to spread their wings. Maybe, Indians were very pious and hence could never fathom the excessively crooked nature of their invaders. The invaders came from areas where bare survival was a struggle, and so when they saw the unprotected treasures in India they looted. Sadly, very few Hindus resisted. The Portuguese occupied Goa and they ruthlessly converted Goanese into Catholic Christians. The Dutch, the French, the Mongols, the Turks, and many others came to India, which was like a house without a master, and an open door, and tried their luck. The most successful were the Mughals and the British. Their tales of torture surpass all of the worst examples in contemporary history. The puzzle is how they succeeded by continuous false propaganda against the docile Hindus and their culture. Even today foolish Hindus still believe that the Mughals and the British were very pious and they ruled Indians, as Indians were unable to rule their own country. These stupid, ignorant, and indifferent Indians need a detailed lesson in correct Indian history. The history written by Congress Party is as perverted as its leadership.

The worst to hit the Hindu culture was the policy by Lord McCauley. It is said that after a serious survey in India, he found out that the Hindus survived the Islamic onslaught because of the ingrained culture of the gurukuls. He estimated their numbers in thousands. And he advised his bosses to destroy these cultural centers, by promoting the Christian education system which was designed to produce obedient slaves or what they called babus. He *succeeded* to such a level that even after two hundred years of occupation and subsequent seventy years of so-called independence we are still slaves of the convent education. (Though most students and their parents do not even know the correct meaning of a convent school.) He has successfully polluted the minds of several generations of Indian kids and created an inbuilt awe and need for English so much so that people who do not know English, nurtured an inherent inferiority complex. English. The brown sahibs are more dangerous than the original version. The new combination of the eastern and western traits culminated in the overall behavior of the brown sahibs. Sometimes they were stauncher than the original sahibs. *Their ridicule of their motherland was rabid.* They tried very hard to disassociate from all that was Indian and more so Hindu. That was the irony! Even today in India such people who abuse and denigrate India are in plenty. Sadly, the high places in Delhi are full of them.

The worst disaster to hit India was the hotchpotch and confused Congress Party reign after 1947. At least we think that they were confused! But maybe the clan of Nehru's, had a *clear-cut plan* of destroying India by way of creating Kashmir, languages problems, regional divides, weak military, absolute chaos on the geographical borders, autocratic rule in which all those dissenting voices were ruthlessly silenced, appeasement of their people, partial treatment to Pakistan and so many such inexplicable blunders. The authors of the books "The Untold Story", "The Himalayan Blunder", and "Between the Lines" have given us the details which bring tears to the eyes of those who love India.

Subsequently, when India started to re-establish itself after the seventies, the darkest periods of emergency, assassinations, nepotism, mass-scale corruption, and selling out of the gold, the devaluations of the rupee happened. India was ruled by people of questionable origins and character. **Their decisions were at best popular, very rarely proper.** The experiments of the mixed economy, half-baked socialism, extreme hatred for the Hindus, distorting the history, cloning a culture of nepotism, committed judiciary, and control over the print media, have created a weak mindset of Indians. Self-esteem is buried far below the soil.

The ugly mystery of congress rule was never unraveled, but the grapevine was very ripe in which everything was very clear.

The irony of India is most of the pseudo-intellectuals cannot support her cause. All intelligence if not used in the interest of the nation is as useless as a mirror in the hands of a blind person. Sadly, these people are blinded by hatred, disregard, and immense faith in some recent tinpot idealism. They do not have anything worthwhile to replace the present-day system in India but they oppose it for the sake of opposition. The hatred and the vested interests of the Muslims *and the Christians can be understood as their way of serving their religion but the stupid acts of the Hindus cannot be explained. Especially those from JNU,* AMU, Jadavpur, and such centers of excellence are major factors in the overall defamation of India. Sadly, these people have misused their extraordinary intelligence for the benefit of the leftists, Pakistanis, and other religious strongholds. Probably, some of these intellectuals advised the people in power to impose emergency, cut the defense budgets, stop manufacturing in India and import from outside, especially from China, to increase the impact of reservations, increase the subsidies on papers only, never in the practice, to do so many things, not in the larger interest of the nation. their number in the government was consciously increased in the administrative services and the judiciary, Today, if *someone wants to clear* the mess, he would be very highly stressed and it may take a complete generation to wipe out the evil effect. And even more, he is successful at the physical level, the deep impacts on the psyche of the unsuspecting Indian youth would be there for centuries to come. If any act, any preaching, any association, any religion, any sect, any ism, any *anything* in India is creating self-doubt in the minds of the youth, then it is worthless. The nation is always first, always, and forever.

When we think of our country today, we feel we are in a unique position, we are the only ones who face unique problems. We feel wrong if we feel so.

In Dwaparyuga, when Shrikrishna was active, we had similar problems. The situation was so bad that many kings were ruling with absolute power. There were holy alliances and there were unholy ones. It is described as the Rajya of Adharma. So Shrikrishna wanted to re-establish the Dhramarajya, where people would once again live in peace and without fear. Kings like Jarasandha, Rukmi, Shishupal, and even there was Prati Shrikrishna (read as duplicate) were the main reason for the adharma. There was chaos, and each king wanted to be the supreme leader like the king of gods, Indra.

Shrikrishna was aware of the chronic problem of invasions in his comparatively small kingdom of Mathura. Jarasandha had attacked Mathura seventeen times, and though he was defeated every time by Shrikrishna and Balram, it was a heavy burden on the residents of the kingdom. Every war was a loss of revenue. Hence, Shrikrishna decided to move to a distant place in Gujrat. Why and how he selected the Gujrat as a possible alternative for Mathura is a study in social engineering. It was never an ad-hoc decision, but it was after a lot of deliberation and thinking. It was not surprising that the entire population followed their leader Shrikrishna without fear and doubt. Shrikrishna was probably the first person in history to have constructed a brand-new city on the reclaimed land from the sea. He was helped by the architect, developer, and contractor of gods, the famous Vishwakarma, who created a marvel in the form of the golden city of Dwarka. Dwarka became a symbol of prosperity, peace, and a happy populace.

Once Shrikrishna settled in the new city of Dwarka he looked into the remaining parts of Bharat. He could see the fall of the Dharma and the resultant chaotic conditions. He decided to re-establish the best Dhramarajya, something similar to the earlier ones like the Ram Rajya. He was in search of some deserving people. Upon his survey, he could find the two most likely families in the Kauravas and the Pandavas. He was also very distressed when he was informed that the Pandavas were eliminated in the fire at the lakshagruha. He was sad but somehow did not believe in the news. He thought that they would be alive they would visit the swayamvaram of the most beautiful princess of the Panchal kingdom, the daughter of king Drupad, and the one who was born out of a *yagnavedi,* Draupadi. When he saw the Pandavas as Brahmins, he told his brother Balram and explained why he thought so. He was convinced when one of the brahmins got up and shot the arrow through the eye of a revolving fish rotating above, looking into a pot filled with oil.There was a war in which the Kshatriyas wanted to kill those five brahmins. They could not do so. They were very heavily defeated by the brahmins.

That was the first time Shrikrishna saw his cousins. He liked what he saw. He went ahead, followed them to their home, met his aunt Kunti, and promised Pandavas that he would be with them in thick and thin times. He should be in his thirties or slightly less or more. He struck an immediate bond with the third brother Arjun, and their friendship blossomed throughout the rest of their lives. Shrikrishna helped the Pandavas in creating the as beautiful city as Dwarka and named it Indraprastha, near present-day Delhi. It was so magical and magnificent that the entire Bharatvarsha was either proud or jealous of the new kingdom. The topping was in the form of the May Sabha. A version of a magic house full of tricks. Little did they all realize that one of the tricks would be one principal reason for the latter war. It was incomparable and it hit the Duryodhana like a bolt from the blue. It is said that after he saw the prosperity of his cousins the Kauravas prince lost his sleep, and was reduced to a haggard person. He was burning with hatred and wanted anyway to destroy the Pandavas. He wanted his revenge. His anger was kept burning bright by his uncle Shakuni who was himself very unhappy over Gandhari's marriage to a blind prince Dhritrashtra. There was one more in the form of the Karna, who was wounded, confused, and wanted to always prove that he was as good or better than Arjun. Add to this list the Dronacharya, the Eklavya, Shishupal, Rukmi, Jayadrath, and many others who were either defeated by Arjun or Shrikrishna. All of these came together for evil reasons rather than any justified ones. Probably, their logic was the end of the Dwaparyuga and it started the farthest time from the Dharma.

The unholy alliance in which some people had bruised egos, was headed by the Dhritrashtra, who was never crowned because he was blind. He somehow accepted his lots as his fate, but he always wanted that his cunning son must be the next king of Hastinapur. Dhritrashtra knew in his inner core that the Pandavas were better in every respect but could never be magnanimous in his approach towards the progeny of his departed brother. In the whole assembly in Hastinapur, there were some sane and wise people. Like the Vidur, the only brother (Yuyutsu) of Duryodhana who opposed the stupid acts of his brothers. He fought for the Pandavas.

Revenge was the only reason for the existence of all these people. Nobody cared for anything else. They were very unhappy inside, hence frustrated. They could not tolerate the smiling face of Shrikrishna but they had nothing which could help them defeat Shrikrishna. They tried many times and every time they were beaten. So, while they were licking their wounds they used to get together and try again.

Shrikrishna was very aware of such people and the damage they could cause to the nation and the religion. He was also aware of the fact that the common people were indifferent and unconcerned about the national interest. Probably the conflict of being good, the ego of forgiving, over-dependence on some outside forces, blown out of proportion impressions about self, hating someone for no worthwhile reasons, or simply being stupid was in that era also. The typical mentality of the Indians is very old which restricts them from doing something for the nation. Future invasions could happen because of this excessive tolerance, "*it does not concern me*" attitude, and "me before the nation." Moreover, they always felt that either the king should do everything and the population should be left sitting idle with hollow criticism or that God should be full time working for the upkeep of the Indians. The tendency of blaming the god or the king (read government) is still very rampant and acts as the worst factor affecting progress.

Each character in Mahabharat is so true and close to present-day life that one can almost identify someone close to that in the epic. **The question to be answered is what Yogeshwar Shrikrishna would have done to solve the present-day problems of the Sanatan dharma and the Bharatvarsha.** The complications created by stupid decisions, the hatred by the other religions towards the Sanatan dharma, and the indifference of the Hindus towards their cause, seem without answers. Can the wisdom of the Geeta, Uddahv Geeta, really help any willing Indian to overcome the shadows of the evil forces on the Bharatvarsha? Can we be straightforward enough to accept our follies? Would we ever change our ways or we would continue the downslide irrespective of the fact that we are probably best equipped to rule the world amicably? What are the best counters to the stupid concepts of excessive ahimsa, pseudo-secularism, communism, confusion due to the distorted history, enforced inferiority complexes, the partial treatments of Hindus, ever-divisive propaganda, the increasing influence of Islam and Christianity, the disappearing culture of the Sanatan dharma, and many such factors constantly haunting the hapless Hindus?

The first change has to be in the mindsets of those Hindus who think that they are unfortunate to be Hindus. The rest of the Hindus have to get rid of such people or their attitudes. They cause maximum damage to the cause of the re-establishment of the Sanatan dharma. People from other religions whether converted in India or from outside are more or less known to disturb the Hindus, and their responses are normal. What hurts the Hindus is the ignorance of its people and their mis-concepts about Hinduism. They have gone so far off the track, that they *do not* matter really. But we cannot let them go away. We have to bring them back to the main fold and the mainstream. We have to find ways to answer their queries and convince them that they are fortunate to be born Hindu. We have to find answers to the false propaganda against the Manu smriti, Vedas, and all our revered characters in history and the Puranas.

Rightly so, because if someone wants to change the world, he must change himself. If one wants different results, he must discard the existing ways and find out new paths to reach the desired goals.

We know that if we search, we can find readymade FAQs and their logical answers in the lives of Shriram and Shrikrishna. What more do the Hindus expect to happen than the gods themselves come to earth, mix with the population, face the problems, and solve them? Probably they gave *on-the-job* training to the Indians. There was the problem and there was a solution not only on offer, but they both gave an additional live demonstration. We cannot expect that we keep on *making mistakes* and the gods would come and rectify them. We have to introspect, find references in ancient and recent history, weed out the unnecessary elements, we have to regenerate ways of rebuilding the faith systems, or **else we would be extinct** and we would blame the gods for the same when we would be sitting in front of the gods. All our intellect and wealth would be insufficient to protect us. We have to catalog and be vocal about how we are better than most who deride our religion and us. There were characters like Charka, Charvak, Kanak, and so many others who raised queries and were answered properly.

We have to do the ABC analysis for knowing the threat perceptions to us and the Sanatan dharma. The factors are many external and internal.

The external factors are the nations like Pakistan, China, Bangladesh, Turkey, Indonesia, Afghanistan, and these days even Nepal. We have to understand the changed scenario of warfare. India has to finally understand that Islam and Christian countries have a common target. They want that the wisdom of Sanatan dharma must be nullified and their version of religion must be promoted. They are trying for the last two thousand years.

As against the earlier days, the wars would not be fought on the ground, face to face, with weapons, but we would be facing threats arising out of misuse of the information, software attacks, chemical warfare, biological warfare, satellite-controlled missiles, and the worst as in atomic warfare. Somehow or rather the evident earlier balance of power has been relegated to the backseat and any smart person located in any part of the world can trigger a process that would be irreversible and very destructive. The overdependence on digitalization may prove to be detrimental to the entire mankind and maybe it would be the reason for the extinction of mankind.

Internal divisive forces in India are more dangerous than the external versions. <u>They intentionally use Hindu names to cover up their identities</u>. They are not traceable, they are very widely spread, they are never satisfied by what is on offer, they are controlled by external forces, they are fanatics of both regional and religious kinds, they are followers of some inexplicable and *failed isms*, they are vociferous against the inherent wisdom of ancient Sanatan dharma and Hindu culture, they are united with those who are against the national interest and many other such varieties. Sadly, most of these versions are Hindus, but they are ashamed of the fact. The only people across the world who take pride in abusing their own culture, traditions, and religion are mostly Hindus. Even a country like Russia where the shortest-lived newest<u>ism</u> *called communism* originated, calls itself a Christian nation. Practically, all nations except India belong to either one or the other religion.

If we see through the present-day *isms,* we should look into what Lord Acton has said, about isms and their impacts. He said that isms corrupt people's minds, while power corrupts only its possessor. The potential of the thoughts is very huge and it is proved in the spread of religions. There is excessive stress on the unilateral thinking processes and unnecessary forceful implementation of the secular state has resulted in diluting the age-old and proven Sanatan philosophy in India which had in the past, helped the survival of Hindus against all odds. We are digressing from our value systems and presently we find that we have nothing with which we can replace it. So, we are losers on both accounts.

Shrikrishna has provided relevant answers for many complex and easy situations in our lives in the Geeta. He has punctured the *aham* of a human being and explained that we should not carry the baggage of unnecessary details, for which we are not responsible. The dialogue is on a very high philosophical plane, that it happened on a battlefield is very significant. To speak extempore for about one hour, in the form of shlokas, and explain the whole philosophy of existence and beyond existence is unique. He needed about seven hundred shlokas to present the knowledge on a platter to Arjun.

Subsequently, many have tried to explain the Geeta, the most significant amongst all is the thirteenth-century Marathi saint Dnyaneshwar, who in himself was a divine miracle. Dnyaneshwar translated the Geeta and explained it in a very understandable simple Marathi language of his times. Even one of the greatest human minds like him needed nine thousand couplets (known as ovi) to explain the Geeta. He presented the gist of his creation in the last prayer to the almighty Sarveshwar, known as the *Pasaydaan* consisting of nine couplets, in which he pleads for the peace, Dnyan, and fulfillment of each desire of each living being. It is said that if someone wants to improve the conditions of the present-day confusing world, he should begin applying the principles explained in the Pasaydaan. Dnyaneshwar is worried about the people. But he is more worried about the evil tendencies in the people. He knows that the origin of the pain is in the unjustified desires, he also says that the evil tendency needs to be destroyed and replaced by something more pious so that the good would be more in number. He compares good people to that the *kalpavriksha*, a tree in the swarga, which grants all wishes. He prays for the congregation of such people, who would clean the not-so-good by their mere association. Probably he was one of the first people who were talking about the law of attraction. He was trying to tell us that the goodness of the people due to Satsang can be very powerful. He tells us that the mother loves all her offspring, but she is slightly more worried about the son who is not as capable as his other siblings. She is more concerned about his welfare. She knows that her capable son would be somehow successful and fulfill his duties. But she is very concerned about the wellbeing of that son who would be left lonely, poked fun at, and more likely to adopt evil ways of life so she prays for his *shubh*.

Dnyaneshwar Mauli as he is called, is compared to being the supreme Mata, the mother who cares. He is more worried about the wicked, evil, and lopsided people in society and wishes for the decline of the evil tendency in the people rather than the evil people themselves. He feels that the mere removal of the wicked people would not solve the problems, as the gap created would be refilled with even worse variety. He also says that whatever little gentle, good, noble, kind, and true is in the evil people should outgrow the evil.

What is to be noted is the sweet nectar of supreme knowledge is coming from a teenager, who was persecuted by the people for no fault of his and ostracized by society for the assumed faults of his parents, and in return, he is praying for them and asking the Sarveshwar for the cleansing of their minds. He was so accomplished that at the tender age of twenty-one he sought permission from his elder brother Nivaruttinath, who was also his Guru, to proceed for a Sanjivan Samadhi and probably the only known example in the entire mankind to do so. The Sanjivan Samadhi is a very complex process in which the person voluntarily disintegrates into the five major portions (panchmahabhuta) of the human body such as Prithvi, Jal, Tej, Akash, and Vayu. At the end of the process, he merges with the supreme existence with the Yogeshwar Shrikrishna.

Many others in our country tried to decode the Bhagwat Geeta, prominent were Lokmanya Tilak, Swami Vivekanand, Dr. Radhakrishnan, Prabhupaad swami of ISKCON, and so many others. But the mystery continues and the more one tries to analyze and understand, the more intriguing it seems to become. We tend to understand the Geeta differently in the different stages of our lives. We simply have to marvel at the place where it was narrated, the time of the narration, and the concise clear, and correct contents of the Geeta. When Shrikrishna said that there would be no more original thoughts in the future world after the Geeta we understand why he said so.

In no other book, the significance of the act of karma has been explained so candidly. No person other than Shrikrishna is so clear about why anything is done, the entire mechanics of the universe, the concept of paap and Punya, where to stop and where to begin, and the overall reason for the existence of human beings.

The Bhagwat Geeta in itself is a complete volume of knowledge that is somehow never properly used by Hindus. They use it as something for taking oaths in judicial matters and most of them probably never read it. *They keep it pending for their old age.* Doing so they miss the greatest opportunity to improve the quality of their lives when it matters.

We must also note that Shrikrishna even with all his divine powers waited for the later part of his life to narrate the Geeta. He used a series of filters before he chose Arjun as a worthy listener of the supreme advice. He tested various aspects of the capacity of Arjun for a long time of fifty years (it is said that when Shrikrishna met Arjun for the first time in the swayamvaram of Draupadi, Arjun was thirty years old, and at the time of the narration of Geeta he was eighty years old) before he delivered one of the **most effective motivational speeches** in the entire history of mankind. In the eighteen days of war that followed the Geeta, Shrikrishna was extremely active in directing the disciple, for remaining on the path of victory. It was not a straightforward mission. Many hurdles, ego trips, obstacles, stupidities, tiffs between the brothers, and the excellence on the part of the warriors in the opposition had to be tackled on a case-to-case basis. How well Shrikrishna did it is a matter of great intrigue and practical intelligence.

***

*

CHAPTER FOUR

Krishna-charitra in one shloka.

Krishna-Charitra in one shloka.

Thousands of words in hundreds of languages have been written to describe the *gudh(mystical)* and exciting character of Shrikrishna. It is very difficult to find such a complete and at the same time versatile character in the entire history of mankind. From his birth to childhood to his final day the life of Shrikrishna is unique and beyond comparison.

When asked a question about whether the world is *Satya* or *Maya* the Chaitanya Mahaprabhu said that he was not very aware of whether the world is real or unreal, but the only thing he was certain about was the lotus-like feet of Shrikrishna. That was the ultimate truth for him. The shloka goes like जगत्सत्यमसत्यं वा नेतरेति मतर्मिम I

शरीकृष्णचरणाम्बुजम सत्यमेव न संशय: ॥

-Chaitanya Charitavli

Once, a hardcore communist pseudointellectual and an atheist asked a learned swami, "What do you like in the character of Shrikrishna?"

The Swami simply answered "Everything about him. Each aspect is so much adorable. I think I know him, but as I know more about him, I know that I really do not know him. He is unfathomable, unending, mystical, mischievous, simple, complex, artist, flutist, dancer, warrior, charioteer, larger than the universe, smaller than the ant, as bright as the midday sun, and as pleasant as the moon on the Poornima, he is caring and at the same time he is detached, he is the ultimate Gyani, he is an orator, motivator, developer, and while he knows everything, still he can be as common as you and me. He is without any ego; he is by your side when you need him most. He is fair, sthitpradnya, he looks for the future, he is a great planner, a greater strategist, and the greatest winner always. He cares for his people, but he is very aware of their shortfalls. He accepts you as you are, without any preconditions." After saying this the swami smiled and just walked away from the buffoon, like his Yogeshwar Master, who never wasted time arguing with fools. Shrikrishna very well knew that when one argues with fools, the only person who loses is the one who is sane as the fool has nothing to lose.

Anybody who tells you that he has understood Shrikrishna, get away as far as possible from him, most likely he is just displaying his ignorance. Any one part of Shrikrishna's life is not just happening. It is on purpose, it is deliberate, and each part has millions of followers who study the same for their lives. Some study his *balroop (childhood)*, some his friendships, some his strategies, and some study his management but all such aspects are more for the convenience of the people. The life of Shrikrishna is mixed, multidimensional, contradictory, complex, intertwined, interesting, overlapping, and intriguing.

Many people are confused about where to start to study him. They do not know; what they should do is they should begin at the same moment. Shrikrishna in his Purnavtar is *athang, unlimited* so it helps you to start at any point. *That is* the beginning of knowledge. What is important is that *you start*. You should also remember that when you are by the side of a lake, you drink water only to quench your thirst and leave the rest for the others. Similarly, you should study the life of Shrikrishna only as per your capability and leave the rest for the others. The ocean of His grace is more than enough for the entire mankind, animals, and plants of the known and unknown parts of the universe.

The problem with people studying Shrikrishna is that they become possessive and presumptuous. When they start feeling that they know it all, they forget that they have not even started. The reasons for calling the Shrikrishna avatar a Purnavtar are many and have been discussed at length by many. The best way to <u>study Shrikrishna is to offer you, yourself, your ego, and your consciousness</u> to him and see him as the only thing that matters. Your life takes a twist and changes into something very serene and bereft of grief, tensions, and worries. He takes your life over and controls you without you even realizing it. One simple path is through the Shrimad Bhagwat. It is the complete text of thousands of shlokas in the praise of the Yogeshwar Shrikrishna. One may spend a lot of time here or if he wants, he should know that Shrimad Bhagwat is summed up in four shlokas called *chatur shloki* Bhagwat. What are the four that sum up the entire Bhagwat? They are as follows:

Sri Bhagavan uvacha (said):

1. aham evasam evagre nanyad yat sad-asat param

    pascad aham yad etac ca yo 'vasisyeta so 'smy aham

The meaning of the first shloka:

At the beginning even before the universe I was there, apart from me there was nothing, neither large nor minute, what matters and what does not, the need for creation and destruction, what is seen is me and what would remain after the final destruction would also be me. Wherever there is no Srishti, I am and only I am present.

*

2). rtertham yat pratiyeta na pratiyeta catmani

tad vidyad atmano mayam yathabhaso yatha tamah

The meaning of the second shloka of the chatur shloki Bhagwat is: whatever is present or seen in any form besides me, is a classic example of Maya. It appears almost real, but it is not. It is unreal like a reflection of the real one. Anything without me is of no

significance.
**

3). yatha mahanti bhutani bhutesuccavacesv anu
pravistany apravistani tatha tesu na tesv aham

The third of the four shloka says: Just like the *panchmahabhuta* the five great components of the universe, such as earth, water, air, fire, and space are present in all beings, and at the same time, they are not there, as they all exist without the beings. Likewise, the supreme reality which is me is inside each being and yet not in any of them, as the supreme reality does exist without any of these beings.
***

4). Etava deva jijnasyam tattva jijnasunatmanah
anvaya-vyatirekabhyam yat syat sarvatra sarvada

If anyone wants to know about the supreme power controlling everything moving and non-moving, he has to understand that the all-encompassing and existing everywhere, is the supreme alone. He is present everywhere at all times or even whatever is supposed to exist beyond time and space. He is there during the creation and he would be there after the destruction (pralaya). He is the only and the ultimate truth, the rest is just an illusion.
****

Shrikrishna in the tenth chapter of the Geeta, also says "The wisest rishis or the gods do not really know anything about my origin or my riches, but they are all created by me. I am at their root."

"I am the creator of the world, universe, and the philosophical worlds. Everything originates from me. Those who realize this simple fact get closer to me and worship me."

"I am the best in everything that matters. The best in the Vedas, the best in the stars, the best in the gods, I am the mind which controls the rest of the organs and the body. I am the Shankar, I am the Meru, I am the Kubera, I am the fire and I am also the sea, I am the Kartikeya as the commander of forces, I am the Brihaspati the guru of the gods. I am the Bhrigu, in the maharishis, I am then omkar the best in the sound (*dhwani*), I am the Himalayas, so please know my dear Arjun, I am the best in everything."

Shrikrishna tells Arjun that he should and must have implicit faith in him if he wants to accomplish anything at all.

He also tells us the pathways which we would have to follow if we have to reach him. Bhakti Marg is the easiest and hence followed by many. To be a bhakta of the Yogeshwar Shrikrishna there is no prequalification. There is no need to be extraordinary. There is no need to study. There is no need to be a complete person, people like Surdas, and Sant Gulabbaba, have been blessed by Shrikrishna. They saw him in full blossom and colours the charitra of Shrikrishna which the people with eyes and sight could never do. The vision it seems is more important than the mere physical sight when you pursue the path of devotion. They all became complete just by staying with the Yogeshwar.

Shrikrishna easily moves in all parts of yoga hence he is the Yogeshwar. Whether dnyanyog, rajyog, karma yoga, or bhakitiyog Shrikrishna has complete mastery over each aspect. He discusses each with surgical precision and absolute authority. He is the one who not only followed the dharma shastra but many times created new versions. He was sure that what was right in the times of Harishchandra (in Satya Yug) and Ramchandra (in Treta Yug) would not be sufficient in the Dwapar Yug, so he went ahead and changed the shastra and the overall outlook of looking into the shastra and dharma. When he talked about the Kaliyuga, he went ahead and described what should be expected and how to tackle the fall in the values, the mental crookedness, the moral corruption, and the antinational attitudes. Shrikrishna was the only one, who not just broke away from the traditional interpretation of the shastra but went ahead and created a new way of life. He narrated Geeta and Uddahv Geeta. He discussed, he fought for the rise in the Sanatan dharma. He had probably foreseen the ensuing intellectual bankruptcy in the Bharatvarsha. He had predicted that the percentage of intellectuals would decline, and the herd mentality would increase. The average Hindu in the earlier Satya, Treta and

Dwapar Yugas was much wiser, composed, and clear about the purpose of life, than the present-day shallow approach adopted by people in the Kaliyuga.

Krishna Charitra can be simply summed up in a single shloka, just like the Ramayana. The beauty of the character is the way it fits per the imagination and the intellectual capacity of a person who is trying to understand Krishna.

"àdau devakidevigarbhajananaü gopigrhe vardhanam
màyàputanajivitàpaharanam govardhanoddhàranam
kamsacchedanakauravàdihananam kuntisutàpàlanam
etadbhàagavatam puranakathitam Srikrisnalilàmrtam"

The shloka describes the salient points, and it is said that if you just recite this you get complete salvation. The ones who are always in a hurry can recite this and be blessed.

***

It is imperative that one who wants to know about the character of Shrikrishna must realize that he has a choice. He can believe either in the cheap and popular versions or should follow the proper version. In his 125 years of life on the earth, Shrikrishna accomplished so much that even any one of his would be sufficient to make him the best in the world. One can like the Shrikrishna who was *a Makhan chor,* or he can like the one who killed the Kalia. He can take interest in the one who collected the clothes of the gopis or the one who provided the mahavastra to the Draupadi, in distress. He can call him a Ranchhoddas, or he can see the extremely smart strategist in Shrikrishna. He can talk about the Raas-Leela or he can talk about the salvation of sixteen thousand one hundred ladies from the clutches of the Narakasur. He can remember Shrikrishna as someone who allegedly stole the syamayantak-mani or as the one who brought it back by fighting one of the mightiest persons the Jambuwaan. He can remember him as a negotiator or as a failed envoy. He can remember him as a master motivator or as a person cursed by the Gandhari. He can remember Shrikrishna as a narrator of the best knowledge so far in the world, in the Bhagwat Geeta and also in Uddahv Geeta, or as the one who was responsible for the final destruction.

Shrikrishna does not really care about the thinking of the people, who do not matter on an absolute scale. He knows what he is, what he would be, and who should be his bhaktas.

It is unfortunate that some minor portion of Hindus have doubts, and they display their so-called intellectual observations, without understanding that they are falling prey to the tactics of the very people who want to denigrate Hinduism. These people have to understand further that if the others would have a fraction of the charisma of Shrikrishna in one of their gods, they would have just been so proud. We have to realize that Shrikrishna is the only one who proclaims and proves that he is the only one who matters.

***

CHAPTER FIVE

Shrikrishna, as the master strategist

Shrikrishna, as the master strategist

The unwritten rule in the life of any strategist is that people should listen to him. Otherwise, the best laid-out plans bite the dust, if the people around do not trust the strategist. One more thing is that the followers must know that if they do not do things in the way, they should, the strategist would do them in a better way. The plan, its narration, its delegation, and the final execution combined together with a review and course correction make a strategy. The execution of any strategy needs time-to-time scrutiny and course correction, or the strategy does not yield the desired results. Shrikrishna was a real master in all these aspects, hence his success rate was very high.

Shrikrishna as a person was simply magnetic. If he was around nothing else mattered. Nobody else mattered. At the same time, he was one in the group. He was very complex and yet very simple at the same time. He could be with you and a ready smile on offer in the most difficult times. His comforting presence of him was probably the most reassuring thing in the lives of the Pandavas. He was the unifying effect in the camp.

He was the one who enjoyed the complete trust of his people. The people around him were so sure about his capability to overcome any problems due to any reason or sometimes even beyond reason. It was simply there, it had nothing to do with age or experience. (Psychologists call it an aura. Some have exceptionally powerful auras with a spread of more than twenty feet. They can control people in that area without any coercion.) He was merely a kid when people in Gokul were dependent on him for his wisdom. They were beaten to the dust by the oppressive regime of their ruler Kamsa. Their morale was very low. They were terrified. They were physically, mentally, and psychologically reduced to a bit more than slaves. Their lands, animals, and even wives were not safe. But sadly, they believed that someone divine intervention would come and rescue them from their awful lots. (Sadly, _the same weird logic continues even today_). There were flashes of Shrikrishna's divine power but they did not feel so as he was so much like all of them. Whether it was the annihilation of the asuras, the cleansing of the river Yamuna, the epic decision of worshipping mount Govardhan, or even the commercial decision of not supplying milk to the capital Mathura had some deep-rooted logic. It helped the common downtrodden population to re-establish some self-esteem in their own otherwise non-descript existence. Shrikrishna had an uncanny knack for converting the depressing liabilities into some encouraging positives. He had to convince the common Gopas, that they are doing something worthwhile and that they do matter in the overall picture of the State. (_Something similar was attempted by the great JP, the legendary Jai Prakash Narayan in the Emergency years and we could see the results. Whenever the common man is shaken and woken up from his slumber, he can achieve the impossible. What happened later, in 1977, was a miracle. When JP died, the movement was diluted with the usual ingredients like greed and lust for power. It is a matter of regrets. The emerging leaders then were allured by the Maya of the power, corruption, and the love of the family. They in plain words betrayed the trust of the people, which proves that the induction effect of the larger-than-life people may last a little longer but it does get eroded. Such people shamelessly joined hands with the same Congress Party, against whom they partnered with JP. JP was too straight and too patriotic for their ulterior designs of grabbing power. JP had nothing to gain and nothing to lose as compared to his followers. They are_ *still cashing on their nearness with JP. Now their second generation is reaping the benefits.)*

After Shrikrishna killed Kamsa, a major part of his Avatar-Karya was over. He could have very well gone back to his Vaikunthalok, but he did not do so. He must have realized that killing one bad man would not solve the longstanding problem of the *timid* mindset of Hindu people. They depended heavily on someone else to provide solutions for their problems. What is to be noted is, this was much before the promise of *'yadayada hi dharmasya'* was later made by Shrikrishna in the Geeta. One more logic was so deep-rooted that every time the load of *paap* becomes unbearable, the mother earth (the Prithvi), pleads before the Sarveshwar to get rid of the bad people. (It is haunting the Hindus even today. How else you can explain the slavery of one thousand years? Waiting for someone, to rescue you without doing something, is inexplicable nonsense. Even after the Narsimha, Parshuram, Shriram, and Shrikrishna the Hindus still do not understand the simple logic of being prepared and retaliating for self-survival. Stupid governments with their even more stupid policies of nonviolence, cuts in the defence budgets, leaving the border areas undeveloped and claiming that it would be their first line of defence, issuing lathis to the army, and many more such amazing and depressing acts must be deplored. How the Hindus who were always in larger numbers than the invaders succumbed to the rule of foreigners is a matter of research, if it helps in igniting the spirit of self-esteem is to be seen. Or else the Hindus would be driven out of their own nation, in the near future.)

Nothing was different from what it is today, as far as the social situation is concerned, when Shrikrishna was born. The faces of the oppressors were different but they were there in full force. There were the people like Jarasandha, Narakasur, Salva, and many others for whom the lives of the common man were of no value. They terrorized the Praja beyond logic. The daily rituals of the common man were just to pay the exorbitant taxes and learned brahmins and the *rishigan (a group of sages)* were simply killed. The pressure was too much, and the rules if any were changing for the worst by the day. There was a clamour for declaring the *king* as the ultimate god. What is to be seen is the same logic had been there when the avatars of Narsimha, Parshuram, and Shriram had happened. Particular demons like Hiranyakashyapu, Ravan, Kumbhkarna, and so many others were nullified but the tendency was prevalent. As soon as the Praja was provided the respite they just relapsed into their nonsense, sure in the knowledge that they have a permanent staff in the form of Vishnu, Durga, and many other Gods who helped mankind. *(Even today the Hindus are making the **same stupid mistake**, they look for someone up there, to rescue them. If someone amongst themselves is trying to help and retrieve the lost ground, they are not helping him. All the Gyan (wisdom) accumulated over the centuries is not enough for them to energize and start the "do phase." They are doing what should not be done. They are **putting "self"** before the nation. Others are working slowly to displace the Hindus, and are successful. Earlier in history, it was nations from where the Hindus were displaced or converted, now it is the turn of the states in our own nation.)*

Before we go deep into the strategy planned, designed, and executed by Shrikrishna we have to think about what is a strategy. Two words are extremely important in the concept of strategy. Both words, whether the strategy or tactics, in modern management systems, are borrowed from military planning. So, maybe they are about a thousand years old. To oversimplify the matter strategy is the plan for the long term, (about three to five years) whereas the tactic is more mid-term, and may be from a week to a quarter of a year.

When we study Shrikrishna we are simply amazed by his intensity towards data collection, research, analysis, and finally the application of the plan to a certain pre-decided success. What is even more amazing is that Shrikrishna could repeat his great winning streak over a long period of time. From the age of merely eight years to his final call of leaving the world everything he did was planned, strategized, and well-executed.

After he shifted to Dwarka, which in itself was a great strategic decision. It helped him get rid of the constant threat of the invasions of Jarasandha and helped the residents to develop in trade and be prosperous. When he was left with some peace, Shrikrishna took a stock of his *avatarkarya*. He found that his job was half-done. The major job of the re-establishment of Sanatan dharma was not properly addressed. So, he started to look for people, whom he could help and get the work done. Before he did anything, he was clever to find a suitable base in the religious scriptures. He found correct justifications in the religion. He was a master manager as he always managed to get what he wanted to be done by some selected people. Following the same rule, he found out that he had to support the Pandavas to get his long-term objective of re-establishment of the then declining Sanatan dharma. Shrikrishna was aware of the major blocks, both material and the men, who were restricting Arjun and other Pandavas, from going all out against the Duryodhana and Kauravas. The older people like Bhishma, Dronacharya, or even Karna were mighty and wise but with their heavy baggage of various instances in the past. They were powerful but they did not have the courage or conviction to stop Duryodhana and Dhritrashtra. They mostly mumbled when they were required to order in a firm voice and tone. They could never ask the father and son duo to stop doing what they were so shamelessly doing to their family. Bhishma, Dronacharya, Krupacharya, and Vidur, were larger than life but they had big *feet of clay* and could not rise above their obligations. They were the slaves of their egos, and compulsions and hence they could never help the right side of the dharma. They flaunted their past and found justifications to help the side of adharma. And their inaction. *(Even today, we have such people who are very highly educated, and wise but kneel in front of the most unlikely, unscrupulous, and unsuitable antinational people with questionable origins, that too against national interests. Sadly, such people occupied high places.)*

Shrikrishna never wanted to leave anything to chance. So, he planned with all variables in mind. He even had the weaknesses of the Pandavas in his strategy. He was aware that keeping the Pandavas together was his greatest challenge. Staying together, but on only a physical level, is sometimes more dangerous than open division and opposition. (We as Hindus must know this better than any other community. We have so many hidden enemies who are on the prowl to destroy our country.) One can plan for open division and known enemies, but internal mental strife is more deadly. He went out of his way and spent quality time with all six members of the chosen family of the Pandavas.

Shrikrishna was very clever and never shared unnecessary details with people. Need to know basis was probably started by him, he also believed that the undisclosed strategies are more likely to succeed than the hyped ones.

Shrikrishna was very aware and alert throughout his life. He realized that during his lifetime he had created a great number of enemies. Every king defeated by him, every orphaned prince, and every spurned female was a potential danger to him. He was also aware that all of them would get together to kill him and his illustrious brother Balram.

We would begin at the early stage after he had killed Kamsa. He had to counter the mad rage from Jarasandha, the mighty king of Magadha and also the father-in-law of Kamsa. His two daughters were suddenly reduced to being widows from the aristocratic lifestyle at Mathura. Jarasandha took it as a personal affront. He was living for revenge. He was powerful, was very well-connected. It is said that he attacked Mathura eighteen times and was defeated every single time, by the duo of Shrikrishna and Balram. Shrikrishna realized that the cost was too heavy for a victory against an enemy like Jarasandha. Balram was very brave but not as worldly clever as Shrikrishna and he knew it. He accepted the leadership of his younger brother. After defeating Jarasandha, sixteen times or so, he was livid with Shrikrishna for the younger brother always let Jarasandha slip away alive. So Balram reportedly asked for the reasons. Shrikrishna, in his inimitable style, may have said 'You know *bhaiyya*, for sure that I could easily kill him or any other person, but he has to continue living for a purpose. Every time he is defeated, he goes back and rebuilds an army of evil-minded people, then attacks me. He serves those bad men on a platter to me. In another case, we would have to search for them in the entire Bharatvarsha. They all come here and get eliminated. As far as Jarasandha is concerned he is *more in pain when he is alive* than he would have been dead. The pain, of being unable to do anything to me and you, actually disintegrates him. He is just a pawn in my overall game.'

Balram nodded and as usual accepted, and so did the rest of the Yadavas.

Shrikrishna was very patient and probably because of this single character he did not pay any serious attention to the chaos in the country until he established a superlative empire in the present-day Sourashtra, Gujrat, with its capital at the city of Dwarka, far away from the constant threat of Jarasandha. He fortified Dwarka and created an invincible and enormous army under the name, Narayani-sena.

Most of us have a set idea about the reasons for the Mahabharat war. We feel that the war was for deciding the throne of the Hastinapur, for the property disputes, and maybe due to the infighting in the family. If you dig slightly deeper, you would find that those who were involved were inadvertently involved in a much greater tussle. The perennial and still ongoing tussle between the old and the new.

The slightly older and orthodox and rigid sect or division followed the Bhrigu Muni, hence called Bhargava, and the other sect or division followed the Narayana hence called Narayani. Narayani represents a more vibrant, flexible, and somewhat modern way of leading lives. Bhargav's followed rules very rigidly. They were not a sort of inclusive group, they had a fixed view of who, when, why, and even how. On the other hand, the people who followed the Narayani way were ready to change and adapt. Shrikrishna was leading the Narayani people. Like a stagnant pond in which the water is rendered stale and non-potable, the culture also craves change. Those who could change and adapt survived, while others perished.

The Narayani usually were in fewer numbers. They asked questions and pursued the ones in control for the answers. They probably believed in asking why and how, so naturally they rubbed many powerful people in the wrong way. They were used to swimming against the currents so they became strong. They were with limited resources. They were studious and could be very good debaters. They were also aware of the slow rate of change. Shrikrishna was the leader of such people. He was always on the lookout for people who would be ready to take the battle. He was very pleased when he met Pandavas. They were almost customized for the job. They were good but were very apprehensive after their traumatic childhood, and their unwelcome presence in the kingdom of Dhritrashtra. They were better than the Kauravas but not as good as the combined opposition of the Kauravas along with extraordinary people like Bhishma, Dronacharya, Krupacharya, and even Vidur.

So, when the Pandavas were in destitution and without any worthwhile resources they had their lucky turn of destiny. They came in contact with the almighty Shrikrishna. The mere contact with him worked like a *paras* stone (*the stone in western philosophy is referred to as the philosopher's stone. With the name* lapis philosophorum, *the stone was supposed to have mythical powers to convert ordinary base metals to gold or create the elixir of life*). Their life changed for the better in his presence. He was liberal in helping them.

The most important aspect of his association with the Pandavas was his role in planning for the war which he knew was inevitable. The Pandavas were not even aware that they would be playing a major very part in the overall strategy of Shrikrishna. He asked Arjun to go around the Bharatvarsha, get some divine astras, and more importantly get some friends. He developed very good relations with the Gandharvas, the nagas, the tribes in the jungles, and many such people who were never taken seriously by the

Bhargavas. Shrikrishna was aware of the *lacunae* in the Pandavas. But he was *sure* of their culture and morals. He was sure of their obedience. He wanted it to be formalized so he arranged for the wedding of Arjun with his sister Subhadra.

So, by the time the war was looming large Shrikrishna had made all preparations he could. He knew his job was not easy as he would not be directly fighting, but he knew his players well.

Shrikrishna was heading toward the total elimination of unwanted people. He could see the polarization of like-minded people who very patently supported the Kauravas. When the armies gathered at the Kurukshetra, it was very much in the favour of the Duryodhana. He had a league of invincible warriors rated as the *Maharathis*. They were practically invincible. They could have won the war but for the shrewd, calculated, and quite a few times even ruthless strategy of Shrikrishna. Right from day one to day eighteen, Shrikrishna helped Pandavas to get rid of severe problems. The elimination of the likes of Bhishma, Dronacharya, Jayadrath, Shakuni, Karna, Duryodhana, Dusshasana, and many others needed a dedicated strategy. As if the problems from the enemy were not enough, Pandavas also created issues due to unnecessary ego trips. The tiff between Yudhishthira and Arjun, the impulsive vow by Arjun after the killing of Abhimanyu, and the ego trip of Dharmaraj created a homemade variety of complex problems. Every time some smart practical solution was needed which he provided. the additional unnecessary headaches were created by the impulsive behaviour of the Pandavas for Shrikrishna apart from the usual on-the-field hassles. It was the extreme patience combined with a pluck that Shrikrishna could see through the Pandavas as the winners.

Shrikrishna believed in stopping nowhere when the larger interest was at the stake. He could cross all limits. He took Draupadi to meet Bhishma merely one day before the war was planned. He asked her to touch his feet. Bhishma inadvertently blessed her as '*Soubhagyavati bhava*' meaning Shrikrishna secured the lives of her husbands.

***

In the actual war, the management skills of Shrikrishna are very evident. Like he never took Arjun to face Bhishma, for the entire ten days initially.

The use of the Ghatotkach, the asura son of Bhima, for neutralizing the Vasavi-shakti, a gift to Karna by Indra, which was kept reserved by Karna for killing Arjun. But he had to use it after Duryodhana and Dronacharya urged him to kill Ghatotkach. Intensive planning is evident on each day of the great war.

He could arrange that Karna would not participate in the war for the earlier ten days. Shrikrishna knew that combined with Bhishma, Karna would form a deadly combination. He also knew that he could not somehow manage or he wanted to avoid the same. He could arrange the use of Shikhandi, to kill Bhishma. The confusion created by the use of the elephant named Ashwatthama in killing Dronacharya, the classical elimination of Jayadrath, and the elimination of Karna, are superb examples of his acute acumen. There are usual objections about whether it was as per the morals or not. This is simply useless as the *neeti* is expected to be followed **by the good people and for the good people** only. In the words of Samarth Ramdas, it is described very correctly. It says that as per the neeti shastra when you deal with crooked, behave crookedly if needed, arrogant can be tackled by counter arrogance, the mischiefs to be tackled by mischiefs, and there is nothing wrong in it.

'dhata see dhat, uddhata see uddhat,

Kahtnatsee khatnat agatya karave'

Samarth Ramdas.

No Sanatan scripture *prohibits* anyone from using rough tactics when they deal with ruffians or when they deal with people who are bad, without integrity and are ready to backstab. It is useless to show any consideration to such people. In the interest of the nation and the dharma, you **must eliminate** them in any which way possible before they damage your national interests. That himsa (violence) is better than the ahimsa of the weak. It is referred to as *Vadha*. And it is rated very high in the dharma.

None of the people who were eliminated by Shrikrishna deserved any special consideration as they had baggage of their own. If you are good, intelligent, and valiant, but you *do not have integrity* toward your country, you are worth nothing. Such people are more dangerous to the nation as they can plan and execute very mammoth antinational activities.

The end of the war could not be officially announced as Duryodhana was alive and was not traceable. The entire effort of the eighteen days and many years before that would be rendered useless if Duryodhana was not eliminated. That Duryodhana was hiding in a lake was informed to Shrikrishna by his informers. Bhima was also informed separately by the fishermen. They were regular suppliers of rare fish to Bhima. When everything was crosschecked, Shrikrishna went along with the five brothers. Again, Yudhishthira blundered by offering a duel with any of them. But Duryodhana was also an egotist, so he fought with Bhima. Duryodhana was full proof of any injuries due to Gandhari's blessings. Duryodhana knew that he was impregnable due to his mother's boon. Apart from his thighs, he was immune to any hits by gada. Shrikrishna indicated to Bhima that he must hit Duryodhana on the thighs. He was eliminated most painfully.

Even Shrikrishna was not ready for the dastardly act of Ashwatthama, Krupacharya, and Kritvarma. After they met the dying Duryodhana and he made Ashwatthama his *Senapati*, all of them were in the hiding just near the camp of Pandavas. They saw an owl who ate the sleeping birds in their nests. Taking a cue from the owl, they entered the Pandavas' camp in the night and killed everyone. Sons of Pandavas, Draupadi's brother, and almost all in the camp in their sleep. It was the lowest point in the history of Bharatvarsha. But, somehow, even today nobody blames Duryodhana or Ashwatthama. It is said that the three of them went to Duryodhana and reported the total annihilation of the Pandavas camp. Duryodhana died as a *satisfied person* with the knowledge that he was instrumental in the killing of the eighteen akshauhini army. One unit usually has 218700 warriors, so about

3936600 people were killed. Thousands of elephants and horses were also killed. He was responsible for rendering the *Prithvi rid of any* worthwhile Kshatriya people.

The act of the villains is not even discussed; it is **promoted as a just retaliation**. Even today we are given the dose of the same illogical logic about the militants in our country. Many theories are promoted about the greatness of all these characters who, when the time came, sided with the adharma. On an absolute scale, you are either a patriot or otherwise a traitor. Sad but true.

Shrikrishna has said that after his Purnavtar, he would not have any more incarnations. As per the properties of each Yug, the Treta Yug was of mantra shakti, the Krut Yug was of knowledge, Dwapar was war or fighting and the Kali Yug would derive its power through teamwork or organization that is Sangh-shakti.

तुरेतायां मंतुरशकुतशिुच, जुआनशकुतिः कतृ येगो
दुवापरे युदुधशकुतशिुच, संघशकुतिः कलौ युगो।।

One more thing we have to understand is that even today we Hindus expect the **gods to protect us**. Shrikrishna says that you better organize and protect your interests and survive. But the Hindus still prefer to depend upon the gods to protect them. Why? We conveniently tend to forget that the call to the Shrikrishna or other deities has to be pure, very intense, and truthful. Shrikrishna **is not**... *repeat*... *not* an ordinary servant at our beck and call and he is not supposed to sort our lives and their complications created by our errors of judgment. Certain pre-conditions need to be met before Shrikrishna would consider even helping the cunning people in the society. There is no relationship at all between the puja path, karma kand, and the show-off in the forms of public display of devotion. If we check the list of the blessed by Shrikrishna, we find Sudama, Draupadi, Meerabai, Surdas, only Arjun of the Pandavas, and a very few others of the millions who outwardly prayed for the blessings. They may or may not at all ever qualify for the ultimate merging with the "Vasudev Tattva" and may never reach the Vishnu Lok.

***

CHAPTER SIX

Shrikrishna: As the greatest communicator

Shrikrishna: As the greatest communicator

Right from his childhood, Shrikrishna was with a great ability to talk sense. He could somehow convince people around him without appearing to do so. Communication is always for the person in front and Shrikrishna understood very early that he would have to remove the traditional cobwebs in the minds of the people around him.

The instances of explaining to his mother Yashoda why he was not a thief, how he tackled the situation at Govardhan Mountain, and how he explained why Ugrasen, should be the king and not him, are enough examples of his extraordinary power of communication. How he must have convinced the people in Mathura to leave everything and then shift to Dwarka, to an unknown future is still unknown, but the result was astonishing. Each of the citizens followed him and settled in Dwarka.

Shrikrishna and Balram were always in a discussion over something or the other. They had a great bonding and though Balram was the elder he accepted Shrikrishna as the Karta in the family. It was always Shrikrishna who won the argument but never antagonized his elder brother. Now, we have a saying which says you may win an argument but lose a friend, but in the case of Shrikrishna, he won both. Even if we learn one single thing -winning without antagonizing- from the great Shrikrishna, we would be mighty happy.

In the complex situation after the Subhadra-Haran, almost all Yadavas wanted to fight and teach a lesson to Arjun. They were braying for the blood of Arjun. Tempers were flaying all around, most of them were yelling for their chariots, and some of them were so angry that they just wanted to see the beheaded body of Arjun. The only cool person was Shrikrishna and when Balram saw this he called everybody and asked them to talk to Shrikrishna. What he talked to the angry and out-of-control, Yadav clan is a masterpiece, in dressing down and deflating egos. He must have said something like, 'Do you know anybody better than the Kuntiputra when it comes to handsome look, fame, valor, and achievements, if yes, then let us go and fight Arjun. As far as I know that Arjun can be only defeated by the Bhagwan Shankar. Also think, if you go and fight him, chances are heavy that he might defeat you all. Think about the loss of face for you all. As far as I think we should all go and bring them both back and arrange for a grand gala wedding.' Shrikrishna avoided a major showdown in both parties whom he loved dearly. If he had not intervened may be history would have been totally different. Maybe there would have been no war and Duryodhana would have had a clean sweep in absence of any opposition.

Even in the later days, it was only after the Pandavas had a detailed discussion and approval from Shrikrishna they proceeded with any action. The trend followed right till the end of the Mahabharat war.

Shrikrishna also knew for sure when to talk or when not to. His *mouna,* silence coupled with his enigmatic and mystical smile communicated much more than many people with their *Vani.* One more means of perfect communication he used effortlessly was his *venu,* his flute. The residents of the Gokul were sure that everything was all right if he was playing the pleasant tunes, they were more productive and happier. He always tried to choose the right person for the right subject and the right listener. After the War, when Dharmaraj was absolutely low with the feeling of guilt Shrikrishna arranged an epic meet with the Pitamah Bhishma. The dialogue could happen only due to the planning by Shrikrishna. So many instances from the entire life of Shrikrishna can be cited where the initial objections raised by his people were nullified and they accepted what he had to say, that too without any malice.

Whether it was Rukmi, Shishupal, Jarasandha, and many others who had never seen eye to eye with Shrikrishna, due to straightforward reasons. They could never accept the fact that he was the one who controlled the universe. For them, he was a mere cowherd boy, and he could not match them in the dharma of warriors, the Kshatriya. They were proven wrong many times in the war and in the dialogue, but they were never accepted. We can understand their anger and helplessness but we can never condone their obnoxious behavior. Shishupal was the son of Shrikrishna's aunt. The story goes that when Shishupal was born, he had a lot of physical abnormalities. He had three eyes and four arms. His mother was informed that her son would be killed by the person in whose lap the extra organs would drop down. When Shrikrishna visited his aunt and took the newborn in his lap the organs dropped away. The mother was shocked but somehow, she was able to extract a promise from the Yogeshwar that he would forgive his one hundred crimes or sins. Shishupal was stupid, arrogant and conceited enough to commit nearly ninety-nine crimes before he entered the arena of the Rajsuya Yadnya, and there he crossed all his limits. He insulted Bhishma, abused Shrikrishna in every possible way, and as fate would have it, he challenged Shrikrishna for a dual. Shrikrishna used this event and beheaded Shishupal with the Sudarshan chakra. This single act silenced all the antagonism and apprehension of all the kings at the assembly. They had heard about the killing of Jarasandha, but they still were not ready to accept Pandavas as the right people to perform the Rajsuya. The visual impact of Shishupal running for his life, and the whirring chakra following him must be terrible and it must have drained out any leftovers of opposition in the Sabha. That the rest of the Yadnya could be done in peace was a tribute to the communication

of Shrikrishna, this time though it was the audio-visual type.
***

Shrikrishna could be at ease with young, old, very old, ladies, common people, friends, and others with his measured speech. Never in his entire life had he ever wasted his words. He spoke with logic, references, and effects in the future if his advice was to be overlooked. He had a great style of getting what he wanted to be done and at the same time, the person in front felt that he was in control.

Imagine Shrikrishna in the battlefield of Kurukshetra, right in the center waiting for Arjun to get ready, and he finds Arjun in a deflated, defeated, demotivated, powerless state of mind. Arjun wanted to surrender before the war started.

Think from the point of view of Shrikrishna. He must have been shocked; when he heard, mumbling words of Arjun. He knew that the chances of victory were heavily dependent on Arjun. So, what does he do? He just composes 57 shlokas, extempore, without any preparation, talks for about an hour, and talks Arjun through the depression. He talks about everything worthwhile and motivates Arjun not only to stand up once again but to win the war. There is no example that comes anywhere near to this intellectual discourse which is still studied by intellectuals across the world. For the last so many thousands of years, nothing like the Geeta has been achieved by anyone.

Even though he was such a great communicator, orator, and conversationalist was unable to avoid the great war. Shrikrishna was in the role of the envoy of the Pandavas to the Hastinapur kingdom ruled by the blind king, physically and figuratively. To make the matters worse the king had a deep-rooted complaint against destiny. He was almost neurotic and was surrounded by people who had less concern for their kingdom, but a more unreasonable attitude toward their personal grudges. Bhishma was more worried about his pratigya, (the promise he gave to his would-be mother Satyavati), and Dronacharya was very angry about he was treated by his one-time friend Drupad, father of Draupadi. He wanted his revenge. Moreover, Dronacharya was mentally on the side of the Pandavas, but could not go to their side as he was under the weight of the obligation of Hastinapur. Shakuni wanted the end of Kurukul, as he was cheated by the kingdom in getting his sister married to a blind prince. He had come all the way from the Gandhar region, just to be able to return the favor. He had no compunction of any guilt if he was instrumental in destroying the Kauravas. The other kings were either defeated by Arjun, Bhima, or Shrikrishna. So, most of the people and army who were with Kauarvas were either by default or by compulsion. Just imagine the entire Narayanisena about one-third of the total army, could have turned hostile at any time. If there was any time a choice between Shrikrishna and the Kaurav sena they would have gone back to their own. Due to an inexplicable convention, the Kshatriya king would join the army of the king who invited him first. Shalya the king of Madradesh, the real uncle and brother of Madri fought the war against his nephews due to the same logic. Duryodhana welcomed Shayla and his army in a such grand way and never let him know that the hospitality was from the Kauravas. Shalya was deflated but it seems that common sense used to go for a toss in the Bharatvarsha right from ancient times. The *ego of following the Kshatriya dharma* was sadly more than *following the right way*. It continued till Prithiviraj Chauhan and others. How otherwise one can explain the release of Ghori by Prithiviraj so many times? He may have achieved the following of his Kshatriya dharma but he failed in his duty towards the Bharatvarsha. His one act of illogic opened the floodgates of slavery for a thousand years.

Before we go into slightly more in detail about the role of Shrikrishna as the envoy and as the negotiator we should understand that Dhritrashtra had very cunningly sent Sanjaya as his emissary of peace to the eldest Pandav Yudhishthira. The timing was such that Shrikrishna was not around. Sanjaya almost succeeded in convincing Dharmaraj, about the futility of the war. He told the Pandav king 'Dhritrashtra is sure that at least you would realize the enormous damage the war would cost to the whole

Bharatvarsha. You as an apostle of peace must not allow war to happen. You know that war is not a solution to any problem. Dhritrashtra told the same thing to Duryodhana, but you know how he misbehaves with his father. Sanjaya not only was able to convince Dharmaraja but also the four brothers. He painted such a terrific scenario that Pandavas were almost ready to leave the race and go into the forest and live peacefully.

Shrikrishna unexpectedly reached earlier than expected. He took apart Sanjaya and his logic. But he could see that he was half successful. After Sanjaya left for Hastinapur, Shrikrishna had to use all his skills to bring all the brothers from the gloom cast by the clever Sanjaya. The comparison of their loss of interest (Vairagya) with the variety of *smashan* vairagya *(where funerals happen in Hindus)* was also said to have sealed the issue but only halfway. It lasted right till the end of Pandavas. Thankfully the intensity was reduced otherwise the Yudhishthira would have surrendered and taken to the forests without any fight.

None of the Pandavas wanted that Shrikrishna should go to Hastinapur as a peace envoy. They knew that it would be very dangerous for him and the overall purpose. But Shrikrishna was adamant, and he proceeded to Hastinapur with full preparation and caution. He had his Narayani-sena camping in Hastinapur, he had taken full precaution in choosing who would accompany him to the treacherous Duryodhana. He knew about the plans to capture him and even eliminate him.

Shrikrishna was shrewd enough to have his own catering. He did not even want to drink water from the Kaurav camp. He was straightforward enough in telling Duryodhana why he cannot accept the hospitality, on offer. He was very frank with the blind king. He narrated all the correct incidents. He recounted the scenes at the lakshagruha, the gambling incident, referred to the ugly incident involving Draupadi, referred to the humble demand for only five towns for the Pandavas. But the Kauravas were under the influence of the Kanad, who had one of the most wicked minds in ancient India. So Dhritrashtra was profuse in the sugarcoated pleasantries, but inside he was in full support of the plan of ousting the Pandavas. After all, Dhritrashtra believed that he was dealt roughly by destiny. He seriously believed in the claim of his son Duryodhana to the throne of Hastinapur. Inside he hated the power of the five Pandavas and their allies. He was partial beyond any reasonable means, but he wanted to create an image of a helpless father who had no control over his son. But this was all a facewash. If anyone has any doubts, he should just read the first shloka of the Geeta. Dhritrashtra asks Sanjaya 'tell me o Sanjaya, what is happening on the sacred battlefield of Kurukshetra, what are *my* sons doing, and what are the sons of *Pandu* doing? Dhritrashtra was never in the favor of parting with the reigns to the Pandu, but he was helpless at that time. The nail of the division was deep-seated and he never had any affection towards the sons of his brother. He had never sided with the side of moral correctness. He was cleverly using the policy of good uncle and bad son for so many years, and by the time of the actual war, he had perfected his role. After the war, he thought he nearly killed Bhima in a deathly embrace and then even faked the grief scenario. That the iron statue nearly cracked is enough proof of the maniacal physical strength of the blind king who just plainly hated the Pandavas.

***

The effect of what Sanjaya had to say as an envoy of Dhritrashtra to the Pandavas, just before the decision of war was very long-lasting. He was very successful it seems, so much so that Arjun was at the lowest mental strength. He was so distressed by the thought of killing his near and dear ones that he was sobbing and wanted to run away. Against this backdrop, the narration of Bhagwad Geeta is a classic example of supreme excellence in communication.

Does it mean that Shrikrishna always succeeded in communication? No, even he had his share of failures. That Shrikrishna somehow could not convince the arrogant bunch of people at Hastinapur is one exception that proves the rule you cannot win them all. That his negotiations would fail was a foregone conclusion. Duryodhana was never in the mood to accept one little thing with a possible benefit to Pandavas. Secondly, it also proves that unless someone wants to listen to you, whatever you may do, you are bound to fail. (Recent example is Pakistan).

He failed quite a few times but the most significant was when he went to meet the Kauravas and was supposed to avoid the all-destructive War. He went for Shrikrishna Shishtayee and could not succeed. In fact, it is a lesson for all communicators. You cannot communicate with people with closed minds and full of prejudices. Duryodhana ill famously said that he would not spare land occupied on the tip of the needle. After that, there was no chance to avoid the war.

Shrikrishna may have wanted the war to happen. It would clear the earth of all undesirables. But he even then tried his level best and could not break the cover. The climax came when Duryodhana tried to capture and kill Shrikrishna. Probably that was the proverbial last straw before Shrikrishna proceeded to stay with Vidur, one of the few in Hastinapur, who knew what Shrikrishna was for real.

One more masterpiece of communication was what he said to Draupadi when he met her after the ill-famous scenes in the gambling hall. She was inconsolable, she had lost everything, money, kingdom, and even her pride in herself along with her otherwise *invincible* husbands. She wanted to avenge there and then. She cringed every time she remembered the evil touch of the dirty hands of Dusshasana, she was hiding from the searching gazes of the gentlemen who were occupying the thrones. She wanted the end of her insults, misery but she could not do so. She wanted her friend to take his Sudarshan chakra and wipe them all off the face of the earth. She was surprised and she was shivering with rage when she saw Shrikrishna doing nothing. She was unhappy as she felt her last hope had forsaken her. Her sobs were subsiding, and she was becoming calmer, but it was the proverbial calm before the storm. She was ready to explode.

Shrikrishna consoled her, comforted her, and tried to put some realistic reasoning in her distressed mind. He explained to her the facts, as to why Pandavas with all their might would not have succeeded if they were to immediately launch an attack on the crooked Kauravas. He was himself very livid but somehow controlled. He succeeded when he told his Sakhi Draupadi 'I promise you with all my power, Panchali, you would see the ladies of the Kauravas weeping in deeper grief than your present one. All the vows taken by Bhima and Arjun would be fulfilled. But you have to wait for the right designated time. If I was not engaged in fighting the Shalva, the gambling would not have taken place but even I cannot reverse the *niyati*. So, Draupadi, please listen to me and wait for your time.'

The biggest plus point in Shrikrishna's communication was he always treated people with respect. He had a ready smile, and words of comfort. Most importantly he never used the blame game. When a person in distress approached him, he did not give a dose of wisdom on what and how the person could have avoided. He knew the futility of dispensing the unwanted *Gyan*, which instead of diluting the problem, increased the aggravation.

It is not surprising to know that out of the sixty-four kalas, Shrikrishna learned at the Sandipani Gurukul, one was dealing with composing poetry instantly. Probably, that can explain the instant and the battlefield composition of the Geeta.

Even though he was such a great communicator, orator, and conversationalist he was unable to avoid the great war. Shrikrishna was in the role of the envoy of the Pandavas to the Hastinapur kingdom ruled by the blind king, physically and figuratively. To make the matters worse the king had a deep-rooted complaint against destiny. He was surrounded by people who had less concern for their kingdom, but a more unreasonable attitude toward their personal grudges. Bhishma was more worried about his pratigya, (the promise he gave to his would-be mother Satyavati), and Dronacharya was very angry about he was treated by his one-time friend Drupad, father of Draupadi. He wanted his revenge. Moreover, Dronacharya was mentally on the side of the Pandavas, but could not go to their side as he was under the weight of the obligation of Hastinapur. Shakuni wanted the end of Kurukul, as he was cheated by the kingdom in getting his sister married to a blind prince. He had come all the way from the Gandhar region, just to be able to return the favor. He had no compunction of any guilt if he was instrumental in destroying the Kauravas. The other kings were either defeated by Arjun, Bhima, or Shrikrishna. So, most of the people and army who were with Kauarvas were either by default or by compulsion. Just imagine the entire Narayanisena about one-third of the total army, could have turned hostile at any time. If there was any time a choice between Shrikrishna and the Kaurav sena they would have gone back to their own. Due to an inexplicable convention, the Kshatriya king would join the army of the king who invited him first. Shalya the king of Madradesh, the real uncle and brother of Madri fought the war against his nephews due to the same logic. Duryodhana welcomed Shayla and his army in such a grand way and never let him know that the hospitality was from the Kauravas. Shalya was deflated but it seems that common sense it seems, used to go for a toss, in the Bharatvarsha right from ancient times. The ego of following the kshatriya dharma was sadly more than following the right way. It continued till Prithiviraj Chauhan and others.

Before we go into slightly more in details about the role of Shrikrishna in the role and envoy and as the negotiator we should find out the background. Earlier, when the Pandavas were staying in the Prabhaskshetra, in the *vanparva* of the Mahabharat, they happened to meet the duo of Shrikrishna and Balram. After seeing the plight of the recently rich Balram was very livid and said to Shrikrishna that the old saying about the good people get the better lots than the people who abuse the dharma does not seem true. After seeing the misery of the Dharmaraj who is the one epitomized as the dharma in himself, I seriously doubt the sanity of the dharma. All those old and wizened seniors seating in the court of Dhritrashtra, witnessing the *dyuta*, the abominable scenes in which Draupadi was insulted, the below dignity and animal like behaviors of Duryodhana, Karna, Dusshasana, Shakuni need to be questioned and punished. Their deplorable behaviors cannot be condoned under any circumstances. Balram was not very impressed with the Kauarvas at that particular time, but that was not the case after a few years. Just before the decision of Shrikrishna to go and negotiate Balram says something which is absolutely in contrast, to his earlier stand. This time he says why Yudhishthira accepted to play dice with the known fixer like Shakuni? Why he went on playing when he knew that he was being cheated? Why did he not stop at a reasonable point? Why had he accepted to offer his wife as bait? Shakuni was a better player and he won because of his skills. So, the Pandavas should go to the court of Dhritrashtra and get their share amicably. Balram told Shrikrishna to desist from partial support to Pandavas and see things in their real light. Shrikrishna was surprised but he could see that Balram was the victim of the sugarcoated propaganda and media management of the cunning Dhritrashtra. If Balram did not love his brother more than his recently acquired opinion, it was very possible that he could have even fought against the Pandavas. We have to note that the peddling of falsehood as the truth is an age-old phenomenon, and probably our old-timers were better in the game of propagating the lies. When we know that the communication means were not at all comparable to what we have today, at least we feel so. Dhritrashtra and his cunning clan headed by Shakuni, Duryodhana, and Kanad had a set story to peddle, they used their means to wipe out the ill effects of their deeds. We can find many similar examples in independent India.

Shrikrishna when he went to the Hastinapur court he was aware of the impending failure of the *shishthai (shishtha means gentleman)* but as true professional he prepared his brief to the perfection. He included the injustices dished out to the Pandavas, in their childhood, the lakshagruha, the dice game, the insult of Draupadi, the ghoshyatra, the partial division of the kaurav kingdom in which the worst and uninhabitable portion was given to Pandavas. His pitch was so loaded and powerful that the Dhritrashtra was dumbfounded. Shrikrishna painted the total annihilation and end of the Kurukul that there was a deadly silence in the court. Nobody including the smartest could argue with logic. In end he told Dhritrashtra 'On one side of the possible peace you stand and on the other side the Pandavas. If you want, you can stop the impending war. as far as the Pandavas are concerned I can even in these wretched conditions convince them to forego the war. they must get their own created and the self-earned kingdom of Indraprastha.' Dhritrashtra was lost in the correct behavior and the blind love for his wicked son Duryodhana, but he was saved from taking any decision by his son, who was also figuratively blinded by the hatred towards the Pandavas. He said that he would not part with even that part of the land which would rest on the needlepoint. The matter ended there and with the same, ended any possibility of any reconciliation. Shrikrishna *failed*, but it is possible that he wanted it to end that way.

That Shrikrishna somehow could not convince this bunch of people is one exception that proves the rule you cannot win them all. Secondly, it also proves that unless someone wants to listen to you, whatever you may do, you are bound to fail. (Recent example is Pakistan).

Communication is a process that started after the advent of humans on the planet earth. At least we humans think so. After thousands of years, we are still looking for possible improvements. We are aware that we are not near perfection. Maybe we have to seriously review our processes. If teaching and training for twenty years cannot assure a guarantee of effective communication at least in one language we are following something useless and ineffective.

***

Shrikrishna was a master in nonverbal communication. He developed perfect body language which helped him immensely in his life. He was not born as a classical beauty. He was black, and he suffered for the same. He overcame all handicaps and developed his very own style. He was in today's language parlor- a trendsetter. He used available goods like flute, peacock feathers, local flowers and created a permanent image for himself. He used his acumen and succeeded beyond any limit. His body was oozing with confidence, that stemmed from his training. He was easy, almost laidback, but he could evoke confidence and terror as per the requirements of the situations.

One of the great assets he had was his disarming smile. He could say many things with a smile on his face. Shrikrishna is probably the best use of a simple smile. His smile was childlike, mystical, encouraging, and somewhat erotic if needed.

***

CHAPTER SEVEN

Shrikrishna and Change

Shrikrishna and Change

Shrikrishna is the representative of the change. He created the changes. More often he made the people wish for a change he thought was necessary. He helped a few to accomplish some great deeds if they were ready to change. But at the same time, he accepted their reluctance to change. He managed his show with the ones who went with him but had no prejudice against the unchanging people. He was the greatest exponent of free will.

He represents the Narayani thought process as against the Bhargava. So, every time there is a need for a change, we can look up to Shrikrishna for guidance. We rarely realize that we are the only ones in the entire world to have such a beautifully illustrated ready reckoner for the life.

Indians are a typical society. Of late, it has very limited expectations from their rulers they do not many times even *know* who rules them. No wonder they did not know about the change in the reigns from Ashok to Nehru. It did not affect them. And if it did affect them, they rarely did anything worthwhile. Apart from a few Indians, like Chanakya, Shivaji, and Maharana Pratap rest were sure that the Gods would help them. The worst part is that these brave Indians wanted to live as an independent and in an independent country, but they never received any help from the Indians in the majority. They received ridicule in plenty and an unlimited dose of discouragement.

Any person trying to change people finds it extremely difficult. People get used to their lots. Who knows it better than the gullible Indians? Indians got used to the Buddhists, Jains, Christians, Parsees, Muslims, and their tantrums in the old times. In the modern era, post-1947, they got used to socialism, communism, black marketing, corruption, dirty politics, treachery, substandard services, substandard education, and so many things which should have been stopped right in the beginning. So, the need for the relevant changes is to be first found, then the situations happening due to these changes have to be visualized and then finally put in our everything to transform the present conditions for the better.

Shrikrishna is what we see as an agent of change. He is dynamism personified. He controls the lives of his people while moving ahead. His one act of helping the Agni to devour the forest at Khandav-vana helped in getting the land for the Pandavas which was not used for agriculture. Even in those days, there were laws against the conversion of agricultural land for urban development, *like today. <u>But in those days people obeyed the law</u>*. With the land which was subsequently available and a great developer like *Mayasur* who was allowed to flee from the raging fires, Pandavas could have a city like Indraprastha. It was one of the many changes that helped the tottering and poor Rajya of Yudhishthira to emerge as one of the most prospering ones in those times.

Have you ever thought about the chariot that Shrikrishna controlled for Arjun? If you see the intriguing composition of the *ratha, the chariot,* of Arjun you would be really surprised.

The details are as the chariot was known as Kapidhwaj because of the presence of Shri Hanuman on its flag. It was divine creation and was handed over to Arjun by the fire god Agni after he was satisfied by the duo of Arjun and Shrikrishna in the Khandav-Vana fire. The preceding story is very interesting. Takshak, a king of nag-vansh, used to stay in the forest. So, every time, Agni tried to consume the forest, Indra, the god of rains, drenched the forest with rains. Why Agni did not try at other forests is not made clear by the great sage Vyasa. So, when Agni knew that the Pandavas were in search of land which could be used for urbanization and to build their capital, he requested Shrikrishna to let him burn the forest with the entire flora and fauna. It is mentioned that the agricultural land was not used for the construction.

What followed was total carnage and only a few were allowed to get out of the fire. Indra tried his level best but his efforts were negated by Arjun using arrows and by Shrikrishna using the Sudarshan chakra.

Agni was so pleased and satiated that he gave Arjun his bow the Gandiva, two quivers with an unending supply of arrows (Akshaya Bhatas), and even divine armour. He also presented the chariot designed and made by Brahma himself. The four horses were Saibya, Sugriva, Meghapushpa, and Balahaka. It was a divine gift and was taken back by Agni at the end of the war.

There are two instances when Hanuman appears in the Mahabharata. Both times for some reason. The first time it was for nullifying the pride of Bhima, and the second time it was due to an argument with Arjun. Also, Hanuman had the desire to see Shrikrishna.

Somehow Hanuman and Arjun entered an argument where Arjun stated that he could construct the bridge between Bharat and Lanka and it would be better than what the *Vanar* army had done. Hanuman was not amused. He said 'If you can do so and if your bridge can sustain my weight leave aside the rest of the army, I would be on your flag, making you invincible. If the bridge breaks you would self-immolate yourself.' Arjun constructed the bridge in a few minutes, and as soon as Hanuman stepped on the bridge, it collapsed. So, Arjun made a pyre and was about to enter it, Shrikrishna appeared and asked Arjun to construct the bridge once again. He did so but this time when Hanuman tried his entire might but could not break the bridge. He saw the mixed *roopam* of Ram and Shrikrishna. He offered puja and agreed to be on the flag of the chariot. Hence it was then called *Kapi* (Vanar) *dhwaj* (flag) Kapidhwaj rath.

Once the goals were cast, Shrikrishna crossed all limits when he had to, he never quivered for a moment. He went all out to help the Pandavas, effected a change from poor to affluent, from a normal king to Samrat, from a barren forest land to Indraprastha, one of the most prosperous cities in the Bharatvarsha, and he saw to it that nobody dared to challenge the Pandavas.

He was aware that Yudhishthira was nowhere near when it came to applying *kutneeti*. He was too simple. Sadly, when he was engaged in the annihilation of Salva just after the Rajsuya Yadnya, the unfortunate incident of the loaded dice and Draupadi Vastrharan happened. It is even today one of the lowest and the worst day in the entire history of the Bharatvarsha. Shrikrishna when he met inconsolable Draupadi, after this sad incident, declared the end of Kauravas and anyone else who sided with them. It was the beginning of the end for them.

Shrikrishna was very clear about the limits of the then-prevalent dharma and he never hesitated to alter it for the betterment of good people. He redefined many things including the truth. He changed the way people used to think and made them realize the value of real neeti and dharma.

He not only changed the way people thought but he provided guidelines in the form of the Geeta. He wants us to understand the difference between the ahimsa practiced by the weak and the strong. The ahimsa for the weak is as weak as they are. He wants us to be strong and not unnecessarily submissive to the people who wish for our destruction. Even Adi Shankaracharya, while defining the role of the Gyani people, said '*loksangrah lokasya unmarg pravrutti nivaranam*' means to bring back the people who have been distracted and have taken the evil paths, instead of the noble path and to punish all those who are forcing them from becoming the good people they were, and by destroying the evil to help the good people to prosper is the basic objective of the Gyani people.' The ones who are either complete or nearing completion (purnatva) would remain incomplete unless they take the incomplete men around them to the purnatva. They have to understand that even though they are complete they are staying with a majority of the people who have no inkling of what is purnatva. The complete person is compared to the sun which gives the same bright sunlight to all irrespective of their behaviour. The complete person helps not only human beings but also other animals to live in peace with nature or plants to germinate and grow to increase the beauty of mother earth and to bring happiness and prosperity to all who stay with him.

The Hindus practiced the same philosophy for thousands of years before they were shocked out of their bliss, by the unprecedented barbaric behaviour of their invaders. The slide was too slippery and steep. Before the Hindus could get to understand what was happening to them and brace themselves up for any sort of response, they were on the verge of being annihilated or converted. The fight was quite fierce in some cases while in other cases it was an abject surrender. The problem was further complicated by the decision of the invaders to settle down in Bharat. Earlier, they used to loot and go back to their respective nations. But they must have seen the divided approach of Bharat as a nation and they must have realized that they can stay and continue to loot. Things did not stop there; the invaders also saw the huge potential for forced conversion to their respective religions. They felt energized by the inertia of the Hindus and their inaction for stopping the conversions or raids on their properties. The main influencers were the Muslims, the British, and the Portuguese. The present-day façade of the civility of these advanced nations pales away by the extraordinary excesses in the matters of loot, forced conversions, and forced acquisitions of land throughout the country. They were all helped by the newly converted Hindus, which was sad, to say the least. One thing is sure not many were converted by free will. Many of them tried to resist. But they were outwitted by the sheer cruelty of the invaders and the newly converted ones. It was always the meek choice of life before death.

Somehow it continued with all its faults till nineteen hundred and eighteen, when the whole world was shocked by one of the most illogical and cruel concepts of communism. It was a sort of double blow. The first was the just concluded World War I. Communism as a concept was so half-baked, that it did not survive even for hundred years. On the surface level whether Stalin or Lenin or their Indian versions like Dange etc spoke the most adorable things but, on the backside, massacred poor millions and the worst part is the ones who were massacred never knew what for they were killed. (Now, similar things are happening in China.) Suddenly from 1945 to 1990, half of the world was in the grip of exploitation by the communists. Their idea was *simple: talk* good and *act bad*. In India, it was the worst exhibition of stupid unionism which completely killed the industry in Mumbai, Kolkata, and almost all public sector undertakings. Before you understand the ills of communism you have to understand the difference between the creation of wealth and labour principles. For example, when an idea is conceived and later converted into an industry, who are all there? The entrepreneur, his financer, his manufacturing engineers, and a few others. There is no trace of the communists or the union leaders. They have no role in *establishing any unit or creating wealth*. They wait in the background. When the industry starts making a profit, they move in like a wolf pack and put in their demands, mostly unreasonable. They do not stop at that; they strike deals with management and make money for *themselves* and their party, and happily sacrifice the interests of the labour. If you want to check the facts, please try to find a single poor labour leader. You would be surprised to see the extent of the efforts needed. One more thing the communists managed to get in India is the unreasonable labour laws which put too many restrictions on the industry. The laws rarely talk about the *responsibility of the labour* or *their leaders*. No doubt labor is a significant component of the industry and its production, but labour also has to understand its limitations. So many experiments where the labour leaders were handed over the operations of the sick units of the industry have failed again and again to run the same.

The communists spread misinformation about how the industry would be closed if the labour unites. How the labour force is more responsible for the development, they tell a lot of lies. They have created Naxalites, which is the worst form of antinational activity. They created misguided students in so many universities. They have corrupted the minds of young people about the religion, nation, and natural ethos of Hindu culture. They always support the countries like China, Pakistan, and other countries against the interests of India. The Indian government has never understood the difference between leniency and treason. What the communists have done is a long-term treason in a planned and phased-out manner. Indian government should be warier of these intra and internal enemies than the external ones.

Whenever they were given to run the locked-down units, they invariably failed. They have nothing as a core, yes, they can talk loudly but they are absolutely hollow when it comes to the national spirit. Almost all communist leaders are good talkers but that is all.

Three of the most dangerous enemies which would try to destroy the Hindu way of life and Sanatan dharma are the Muslims/Christians, the communists, and the half-baked stupid people from the Hindu religion. The first two are known and you can fight and plan strategies but the third and the last are the worst of the lot.

For tackling the Muslims and their threat we have to know more about their religion than them. There are people in India who are now challenging everything Muslims say about their religion. One more thing about Muslims we have to understand is that they would take you to such a stage where you would have to fight them or die. In the worst case either you have to convert or die. Please note that even if you convert to one of the sects say, Shia or Sunni, for all other sects in Islam you are still a kafir. You have to understand the futility of converting to either Islam or Christianity as you can never overcome the ingrained Sanatan dharma in you.

Shrikrishna prepared us for the problems we facing today. The origin of the problems is mainly in the way we live, eat, think, behave, and act selfishly. The earth was inhabited for millions of years and was a happy planet. In the last three hundred years, the *advanced* and industrialized people of the advanced world have damaged the earth to its core. We have taken more than we needed, wasted a lot, and destroyed the vegetation, geology, sea waters, and mountains, and now we are talking about carbon balance and global warming. Again, the nations which are responsible for the decay are wanting that the nations which have less should compensate for the oxygen loss, and increased carbon by planting more trees and going back to medieval ways of life. It is ironic, to say the least.

Shrikrishna taught us how to change without unnecessarily harming nature. We live in a world where we strive for more speed, more money, and more than required resources, hence we try to increase the efficiency of the systems. We want more in less time. We are changing but are we changing for the better? Are we growing without any appreciable control or are we developing? To know the real answer, we need to define what is our definition of life. We pride ourselves in developing atomic energy, and we believe that we are very advanced in medical sciences, and maybe we are. But are we developed enough to stay in harmony with our neighbour whether a person or a country? Very early in the present century human being understood that he is standing on the brink of a catastrophe as many people like the son of Dronacharya have got access to atomic and hydrogen bombs. Ashwatthama was a character in Mahabharata who was endowed with so much yet he could not achieve much. He was a brahmin but never accepted as one. He always chose to be on the wrong side. There is a story that he once met Shrikrishna and demanded that he is so complete in being the best in the study of arms and super arms that Shrikrishna must give him the Sudarshan chakra to him. Shrikrishna smiled as always and asked him to carry them to his place. Ashwatthama was very blind with pride so he touched the Sudarshan to lift it. He could not move it let alone lift it so he returned home shamefaced. The story of Ashwatthama ends in the Mahabharata where he stoops down to the level of lowest human existence and kills the sleeping army of Pandavas in their camp. He was not satisfied with the inhumane killings and because he wanted away with the Pandu lineage, he launched the Brahmastra on the unborn child of the dead Abhimanyu. To counter the same Arjun also launched the same. There was a holocaust and as usual, Ved Vyas appeared on the scene and asked them both to withdraw the Brahmastra. Arjun obeyed but Ashwatthama could not as he did not know. Later Shrikrishna did the needful. Later on, when Ashwatthama was at the feet of Draupadi, she somehow could not order the killing of Ashwatthama as he was the son of the Dronacharya and he was a brahmin. But Shrikrishna took away his *mani* (the gem he was born with) and cursed him that he would be roaming till the end of the world with an incurable wound on the forehead. He would be one living example of what happens when a person of *less calibre is given the Gyan he does not deserve.* There is a lesson for all of us. There are many like Ashwatthama in India who would go to any extent to harm the nation.

Every change brings in the positives and the negatives. Before any change is initiated in the system, the system operators must study the present system very thoroughly. Changing the operating system without any worthwhile alternative is a sure way of killing the system. An example is the ever-changing education system in India. The system which worked for thousands of years was changed for some unproven untested system that was bound to fail. Education works on the principle of elimination meaning the better ones go up the ladder and the not so good are absorbed on the lateral sides of the system. Irrespective of caste, creed, and other parameters the only objective of any education system must be to provide the required quality of education. Education is not automatic, and it involved a lot of active participation of the students, teachers, and management. In the last seven decades, the only accomplishment of the governments is the dilution of education and mass production of useless educational products.

How do we get back the standards? Simple! We must stop the <u>compromise with the calibre.</u> No political leader however powerful, cannot create an ounce of intelligence in his institutions. He can fabricate the data, and he can fool the willing inspection and supervising bodies like UGC, AICTE, and medical councils but he **cannot create good students by magic**. It is a slow process, and it would now take decades to reverse the effect of the stupid education imparted in our institutions. If everything that is reported is true, then the quality of the students should vindicate the same in their performances. It is not so. The reports say that only ten percent are employable and that includes the IITs, NITs, and IIMs.

So, what does Shrikrishna say about changing education? In Geeta, he talks about education and how it should be. One has to find out the right context in the system today before one applies the same. It is not advised that one should take words from Geeta and apply them to the present systems. One has to understand that some thousands of years have gone by so the references and contexts would have to be found, analyzed, and even tested before they are applied. The acceptability of the scripture as a practical solution to the current problems does not easily flow, it finds stiff resistance from the sections who do not want to find solutions. The bullet points from the Geeta for the students would be like as below:

1. Student must be sure about the correct reasons for why and what he wants to study. It may not be easy, but it would be the correct foundation. *Why* and *how* are the two keywords from the advice of Geeta? Shrikrishna told Arjun why to fight and how to fight and he won the war. The principles of Geeta also tell us that our lives can also be compared to war and hence we should have the correct strategy. If we cannot understand what to do and how to do then we must get to someone who knows and tells us what to do.

2. Students are advised to understand the concept of change. Whether you are happy or sad, successful or a failure, rich or poor it would change. What you do when things are not going your way *decides* your future. Stick to the basics, and keep them right and things would start to change, and you would wonder

why you were so unhappy over something so perishable. So, if you feel that you are the only one who suffers it is not so.

3. Belief in the systems and self. The self and the system are the two basic components of any process. The self must stick to the system or the procedure which many times is not easy. The discouragements from the people around create self-doubt. Self-doubt is the first weakening agent of the foundation of the system.

4. How to come out of self-doubt? Shrikrishna tells us that meditation is one sure way of gaining inner strength and reasserting the systems. When you are in doubt try to find what you were doing right before you were plagued by doubt.

5. <u>Nobody is perfect but has the potential to become perfect</u>. When anyone is born, he has some tendencies, instincts, characters, dispositions, and even memories of the past life. The god endows each creation of his with a great potential to be a winner. Most of us never stretch ourselves and hence we never reach our potential. We do not use our mental faculties and get affected by useless things, which Geeta calls Maya. Even if we are blessed with a lot of potential very few of us attain the full potential. When we start to ask why we tend to improve. The Vrutti and pravrutti along with Nivruti decide what can a person do in his life.

6. Three wicked things kill the prospects of success. They are Kam- *lust*/ krodh *-anger*/ and lobha-greed. Students need to understand the need to address these issues. There are three more called mada *-arrogance* / matsar- jealousy/ and moh-delusion or the urge to have something. As we all know anger management is a big issue these days. Even anger is studied by our Sanatan dharma. The satvik anger or the anger that is deeply rooted where one cannot rise against the systems like the residents of Mathura before the birth of Shrikrishna. They were angry but could do nothing about it. The arrogance stems from shallow half-baked knowledge. The increase in juvenile crimes, the exploitation of women, and the increase in the business of

pornography originate in the Kam. Greed is what has destroyed our planet. When many nations are looting others when they do not need to. The moh is best explained by the kid in a toy store. He wants everything and in that he does not enjoy what he has in his hands. The man when he grows does the same thing, he does not enjoy what he has but craves what others have and pursues the mirage, the Maya.

7. The changes in our lives can be very brutal or very pleasant depending upon what we are talking about. A girl keeps on changing throughout her life but when she becomes a mother, she undergoes a pleasant change that is incomparable to anything else. The creation inside her changes her completely on the outside and the inside. Her priorities change like never before. It surpasses everything so far in her life. Naturally, a girl is more equipped for impending changes in the future.

The job, location, marriage or divorce, birth or death, surprise, and many such things change our lives. Many of us are not trained to cope with the changes, so we somehow learn to live with the change or get severely hurt emotionally. Management of a change is what Shrikrishna talks about in the Geeta. He highlights the state of a *sthitpragya*, which is staying focussed in the stages of such and dukh. He tells in his shloka *Sukh dukhe same kritva* how to tackle the changes. The students need to know one simple thing, that time just goes on.

Shrikrishna was asked by Arjun to write the same but correct response in one sentence for a person in happiness and grief, Shrikrishna simply wrote *"this will pass too."* So even in extreme pain have faith in the change and try to keep doing the things which you are supposed to do.

1. Some changes are short-lived, and some create an impact for generations. For example, in the last thousand years, people have been forced to change the way they live, and the way they pray by force. Religious conversion by force is one of the

most painful changes that only humans suffer. Other animals are free from this, trees are even happier. The futility of the conversion is best put by none other than J. Krishnamurthy and I just quote from his works. He says *"You can be converted from one belief to another, from one dogma to another, but you cannot be converted to the understanding of reality. Belief is not reality. You can change your mind, and your opinion, but truth or God is not a conviction: it is an experience not based on any belief or dogma, or any previous experience. If you have an experience born of belief, your experience is the conditioned response to that belief. If you have an experience unexpectedly, spontaneously, and build further experience upon the first, then experience is merely a continuation of memory that responds to contact with the present. Memory is always dead, coming to life only in contact with the living present. Conversion is a change from one belief or dogma to another, from one ceremony to a more gratifying one, and it does not open the door to reality. On the contrary, gratification is a hindrance to reality. And yet that is what organized religions and religious groups are attempting to do: to convert you to a more reasonable or a less reasonable dogma, superstition, or hope. They offer you a better cage. It may or may not be comfortable, depending on your temperament, but in any case, it is a prison. Religiously and politically, at different levels of culture, this conversion is going on all the time. Organizations, with their leaders, thrive on keeping ma in the ideological patterns they offer, whether religious or economic. In this process lies mutual exploitation. Truth is outside of all patterns, fears, and hopes. If you would discover the supreme happiness of truth, you must break away from all ceremonies and ideological patterns."*

So, be very careful about managing the change or the changes in life.

The Geeta for the sake of studies can be divided into three parts. Parts (Adhaya) one to six mainly deal with karma yoga *the path of action.* Parts seven to twelve deal with bhakti yoga, *the path of devotion,* and parts thirteen to eighteen enlighten us by way of Dnyan yoga, *the path of knowledge.*

Geeta tells the students to be focused, perseverant and receptive to new things. To adapt is to grow and become successful.

Again, we have to decide what the primary purpose of education is imparted to our students. Is it for a job? Is it for a more comprehensive purpose of making him a decent enough man to sustain the ordeals that life is likely to present him with? Is it for teaching him life skills so that he can contribute to the welfare of society? Is it for strengthening his inner Sanctorum so that he can differentiate between good and evil?

After you decide the objectives like the ones given above or some others as per your need and understanding ask yourself a second question. Is my education system living up to the objectives? If yes find out why and stick with the system and if the more likely answer is *no,* then once again find out why and try to modify the present-day systems.

The desperation of the unreasonable people has brought the world to such a stage where we do not know what to look for. The man stands at the crossroads. He turns to religion, philosophy, and the now a day's psychology for the answers. The questions are very complicated and multifaceted. We cannot satisfy all stakeholders. Does it mean we should just succumb, or we should once again brace ourselves for a better future? If we want a calibrated future, then we need to go back to Shrikrishna and learn the ways he wanted us to live. Shrikrishna wanted us to learn the power of unity and organization. He tells us to unite against evil, or otherwise evil would get us to total annihilation. Evil includes evil men, evil tendencies, and evil intentions. And each of them needs a separate and dedicated approach. The evil intention is the result of the thinking of evil men with evil tendencies. For centuries humans have destroyed evil men in the form of asuras, criminals, and overambitious expansionists. But the present-day situation is similar to those days when these people were there. Nothing much has changed. So, the elimination of evil men and intentions seems a lame way of addressing this problem. If we eliminate evil people today, we have no guarantee that there would be no one evil tomorrow. Moreover, what is evil in one country may be very pious in the other. There is a complication due to the religious angle also. All religions except the Sanatan dharma are pretty recent and they have not yet settled. Also, there is a religious compulsion of increasing the number of followers. All religions advocate no forced conversions but that is very hypothetical. The only religion which has never forced any conversions is again the Sanatan dharma for which it has paid by losing millions of followers to Buddhism, Islam, and Christianity. The present geographic and demographic conditions of the world would never *allow* any nation to settle down. The religion, the colour, and the advanced and backward aspects of human beings would be very severe in the years to come.

For anything to change on the outside much more has to change on the inside. Presently even if one wants to change his inside, he is confused. There are many unresolved issues in each version of religion so one has to be discreet and understand the limitations of religion. After all, religions may cause major troubles apart from racial hatred. If all religions promise equality to all their followers, there should be no clashes in the ethnic sections of society. No religion in the present-day world has any control over the behavioural patterns of its followers. Sadly, the mighty, and most wicked in the religion decide how the gullible followers would behave. How otherwise we can explain so many divisions, cults, sects, and castes, who are ready to slit each other's throats at the drop of a hat. The even more worrying fact is none of these factions are happy even when they get to live their way. The strength of the religion must be measured by its longevity of the same. Religions have their problems, some are naturally occurring, but many are intentionally created to help some faction to become stronger. In the end, nothing survives except of the bare knowledge at the core of the religion.

Going back to the chariot of Arjun it tells us changing of a person on the inner side. People are prejudiced and they are ignorant. It is a deadly combination. How much and how much more in any way possible would lead human beings nowhere as he tends to forget he cannot take anything from this mortal world to the other world. Not even his mortal remains. But he does not understand, again taking an example from the Mahabharata, where so many extraordinary people lived extraordinary lives, but could not take anything with them. The only exception was the Dharmaraj who could go to the *swarga*, with his earthly remains. Plus, a dog. Furthermore, the calculations of heaven are different from those on earth. Those who were very sinful were in heaven and those who were pious were in hell. So, Yudhishthira was nonplussed.

For the people on earth, each religion has somewhat similar concepts of heaven, hell, and earth. Also, there is an in-charge deity for the counting of sins and good deeds. There are similar principles of behaviour, so there should be no clashes between the followers. That does not seem the case. The conflict arises from the argument of point a, *my religion is better than yours,* and point b, due to conversion by force.

Changes do occur in the lives of people in distressed times. In the classic Hindi movie Anand, the doctor is an atheist. But when Anand is about to die the same doctor accepts that he is willing to believe in God if that is going to save Anand's life. There are so many examples where non-believers are turned into staunch believers. It is better to live with faith than without it. It is more difficult to prove the absence of a supreme power than the presence of the same. Life becomes easy, hopeful and there is positivity around you. Prayers give you hope. Life without hope is actually without any drive to do something better. Faith is the driving force behind many impossible achievements. Faith in the supreme generates the all-important initiative to overcome the odds against you. In India, there are so many examples. The Indian youth has very positively learned to fight the odds.

When you learn that many are better than you take the first step to change. Once you decide to change the parameters the expected change appears on your mind screen. Things appear to change for the better. Nothing changes unless you change and if it changes without you, you are out of the frame. Then you are bound to be relegated to some insignificant corner, so better change.

One of the most important things about the changes is the speed at which you make them happen. The surprise element is the winning factor. If your enemies know that you are changing then you would find them more equipped and prepared to fight back against the change.

To effect a change the first thing you need is faith in yourself and your Creator, then you need a plan, a strong iron that will execute the plan, perseverance to go through the difficult times, and strength to do something which leads to the desired and pre-decided change.

For a country to change positively, the leadership must be exceptionally *clean, clear, and correct.* That is the first prerequisite, the rest is redundant. For a nation to rise in the world rankings is a long and arduous process but the downslide can be triggered by a single and simple mistake. That sort of change is unwelcome, and devastating and may take decades to stage a reversal in the trends. Bharatvarsha is undergoing the same process of finding its roots, in the charred fields. Again, the aftereffects of the short-sighted, populistic, partial, and course, stupid policies are very visible and they would haunt us for at least the next hundred years. Recently, countries that, not very long ago, were extremely rich and resourceful like Venezuela have suddenly gone down the drain. One simple reason can be enough.

All such stakeholders can learn a lot from the ancient Indian philosophy of nation-building, taxation policies, asset management, and man management. Shrikrishna explains these aspects in the Geeta. Shrikrishna tells us to change for the better, change for becoming more worthy than what we are now, so that, we are more prepared to merge with his supreme being, which anyway is the only thing we should live for. Rest everything keeps on changing, but for the final acceptance by him.

Once Shrikrishna accepts us, *you* and Icease to be there. You are free of all worldly feelings; you are free of the sukh or the dukh. You are just there as a part of him. You change once for the never changing form of yours. You are eternally happy and with your Shrikrishna. Then nothing remains the same, nothing changes, nothing matters, nothing is created or destroyed, and everything is eternal, peaceful, and full of bliss. Even that does not matter.

***

Mahabharat Before and After Shrikrishna

<u>Mahabharat Before and After Shrikrishna</u>

Mahabharat's story started well before the birth of Shrikrishna. From the great story of Shakuntala and Dushyant and their son the great Bharat to the birth of Pandavas and Kauravas, there were many ordinary and extraordinary personalities. There was Yayati, Puru, Shantanu, Bhishma, and then the current race of Kauravas and Pandavas. We are talking of about seven to eight generations, but there was nothing extraordinary in that sense except the story of Puru and later Shantanu. There were many achievements but they were supposed to be normal for the Kshatriyas. They were in tune with the expectations of what a model king should be.

Everything was going well, Shantanu had the best Yuvaraja in his son Devvrata, and in the entire Bharatvarsha, he was happy that his son was winning wars and was one of the most eligible bachelors in the area. He was even planning to marry him to some beautiful princess.

But then he *saw* Matsygandha.

The extraordinary beautiful girl of the king of fishermen. (There was a substory involving Matsygandha and Parashar rishi. She was rowing the boat in which Parashar was crossing the river to proceed to the Himalayas for some Tapasyaa, penance. He had not had a woman in many years. So, when he saw the Matsygandha exuding her full charm he wanted her then and there. She was very pleased, but she was smart enough not to agree immediately. She put across her arguments. She said that she stinks of fish, so, Parashar by his yogic powers not only removed the stink but made her fragrant like flowers. She was now Satyavati, the *Yojangandha*, (Yojan equals to about five miles) whose fragrance could be smelled as long as miles away. She could sense the desperation and hence she stretched a little further, and she then complained about her losing virginity. Parashar said that she would not lose her virginity. Then she said that people could see them in the act, so Parashar created a dense fog across the river to block any visibility. After all this, he had his share of lovemaking. Parashar subsequently repented from his act but it just proved that he was a human. He did not realize that he was to be instrumental in the recording of history through his son Vyasa, who was born to Satyavati. He was the main reason for the further *continued* Kul of Kurus and Pandavas. He used the Niyoga method to produce Dhritrashtra, Pandu, and Vidur. Again, in the next generation he used the method, very near to the methods like artificial IVF (*in vitro fertilization or test tube babies or the cloning* we use now) for the birth of one hundred Kauravas)

Pandu and his wives were in the forest after a horrible curse by Kindam rishi on Pandu. (Kindam was a very shy person and hence he used to assume the forms of various animals and have sex with his wife) Once he was in the act in the form of a stag and Pandu killed him as a game hunting act. So, Kindam cursed Pandu that he could not have sex with his wives. Pandu would be dead the moment he touched his wives. So, Pandu relinquished his kingdom and proceeded to *Gandhmadan* forest. He assumed the life of a monk. Pandu, Kunti, and Madri were in distress as there was a constant threat of impending and almost inevitable disaster. Pandu had two very beautiful wives and yet he could not enjoy them.

Vyas went there and consoled them. While doing so he also told Pandu about the boon to Kunti by Duravasa rishi. Pandu insisted and Kunti invoked the Yama, Vayu, and Indra to have three sons Yudhishthira, Bhima, and Arjun. It did not stop there as Madri also wanted to have sons. Very reluctantly Kunti agreed to one-time favour to Madri. She called the twins Ashwini Kumaras and had twin sons named Nakul and Sahdev. There is a story that tells us why these things happened the way they were. There is some rationale in the form of previous births, in the Mahabharat. You may believe it or not it is up to you. But to relate these stories in the present-day contexts is a futile and frustrating exercise.

The history of the births in the entire epic of Mahabharata is peculiar, to say the least. It depends upon a view of a person to accept it or ridicule it. It can be a scientific, or mythological miracle. Even if it is imaginary, it is in a class by itself. It shows the practical and rational approach toward the desire to continue the lineage. People were open and transparent about what they wanted and how to obtain what they wanted.

***

After Shantanu saw Satyavati, he became a walking zombie. He was looking pale and sick. Devvrata tried to find out why and when he knew the real reason, he approached the Dashraj, and discussed the possibility of marriage. Later he accepted all terms and brought Satyavati to Hastinapur is folklore and we all know it. He was named Bhishma and his vow was Bhishmapratigya. The question of whether he did the right thing or not is still not answered properly. Except that as he was one of the Vasu's from the Devlok and upon the request from his wife, he tried to steal the Kamdhenu from the Vasishta rishi ashram. He was the only one of the Vasu's who would have to stay on the earth, rest seven would go back to the Swarglok without spending time on the Prithvi-Lok. He was the main culprit and the rest were accomplices. So, like many stories in Mahabharat, we should accept this story also as *maybe it is possible*.

***

Shrikrishna entered the stage of Mahabharat quite late when he was probably in his thirties. He entered the scene of Swayamvaram of Draupadi. The Pandavas already beaten miserably by the Kauravas, in the games of dirty politics were hiding in the small town of Ekchakra. They had barely survived the attempt on their lives in the lakshagruha, that too, because they received a solid tip from Vidur, one of the few well-wishers of them, in Hastinapur, about the accurate timing and the method to be used in the arson. The Pandavas for once acted cleverly and created an acceptable crime scene, from where six bodies were recovered from the place of arson. The Kauravas were happy inside but on the outside shed a lot of tears. They *were outwardly and officially* in grief. The practice of state mourning may have started from this point.

The Pandavas could breathe slightly more comfortably as they were no more hunted. They decided to be *"better dead"* than be killed in one more attempt by their beloved cousins.

The Pandavas were in a bad time right from their birth. (Not so the Kauravas!) They were in the forest for no fault of theirs, with a cursed father, who was living in fear for his life, they were devoid of their rightful regal privileges. After all their father was the ruling king of Hastinapur. But they were reasonably and surprisingly happy even in those dreadful conditions, as they did not know anything about their rightful place in the palace of Hastinapur. After the death of Pandu and Madri, they returned to Hastinapur as poor and unwelcome relatives. They looked almost like refugees and were treated like ones. They were given regal clothes or a palace, but Duryodhana was always there to remind them that they were unwanted. Whatever affection showed by their uncle Dhritrashtra was on the surface level and he never wanted any competition for his elder son Duryodhana. The only real affection was from the Bhishma and Vidur. Somehow surprisingly, the populace of Hastinapur was greatly impressed by the sons of Pandu, which further irritated the Dhritrashtra clan. Right from the beginning, it was *"hate at the first sight"* for Duryodhana toward the Pandavas. Duryodhana was a son of a Samrat in his full colours. He was developing into a classical villain under the supervision of Shakuni and people like Kanad. So, he never wanted any cousins and denied their claim over the Hastinapur kingdom. That in the future, the Pandavas proved better in all aspects of education, morals and culture added fuel to the fire of hatred. Right from an early age, he wanted to get rid of his unwanted cousins. He never made any show of love. He in fact tried to kill Bhima by poisoning and throwing him in a lake. He and his pet brother Dusshasana never missed an opportunity to deride and degrade the Pandavas. Among the Pandavas, the only aggression was from Bhima who in plain words terrorized the Kauravas. Entire hundred brothers were in awe and terror of Bhima. So, every time Bhima pulled a trick it created one more knot of hatred in the calculating mind of Duryodhana.

So, before Pandavas finally met Shrikrishna, they were apprehensive, trying to find their roots, defensive for no reason, affected by the pure hatred of Duryodhana and the concealed hatred of Dhritrashtra. Gandhari was warning her husband of the waywardness of Duryodhana, but the blind father was further blinded by the excessive love of the son.

Apart from their heroics in the passing out competition from then Dronacharya Gurukul, which displayed the expertise of the princes, Pandavas had very little to show to the world. Whatever their claims may have been they were all still at the mercy of uncle Dhritrashtra. They were living in fear of death. Further, the excessively religious-minded Dharmaraj did not help their cause. So, if Shrikrishna had not met the Pandavas their destiny would have been very clear and poor. At the most, they would have served the Kauravas as virtual nobodies and would have constantly faced humiliation. That *one has to fight for his rights* was not in the smallest corner of the mind of Dharmaraj. He was also a prisoner of his mindset, like so many in the epic Mahabharata, and a classic case of personal ego before the welfare of the family and the nation.

Pandavas were not even aware that they had strong support waiting in the wings. As it could be for them at that time, Shrikrishna was too big in status and too far away from Hastinapur. So, he was very much out of frame for the Pandavas. Probably, they never thought of Shrikrishna, apart from the usual sense of awe for a person who had then accomplished so much against all odds. There was no connection at all, even Kunti who never stayed with the family of Shrikrishna, as she was adopted by king

Kuntibhoj. Shrikrishna met them all for the first time in the house of a potter in Ekchakra town, where the Pandavas were hiding after the lakshagruha incident.

The moment Shrikrishna saw them at the swayamvaram venue the wheels of fortune started changing for the Pandavas. From a destitute, poor, lonely, and almost hopeless bunch, they were reformed into a rich, powerful, well-connected, and optimistic bunch of young Kshatriyas.

From that moment everything in the lives of Pandavas was as per the plans of Shrikrishna. In all policy matters, Shrikrishna played a major role. Earlier because of the excessive goodness of their eldest brother they were mostly at the receiving end. The addiction to the fact that *"I am the greatest follower of dharma, I do not speak lies, I am the fairest of all human beings" was hurting Yudhishthira.* And becausehe was the Karta in the family it affected all Pandavas. They were trying hard to find the logic in their eldest brother's thought process but rarely they succeeded. It was most difficult for Bhima, but he controlled his rage admirably well.

The decision of Draupadi to get married to all five brothers was possible only after Shrikrishna told them the story of her previous birth, otherwise, it was going to be a big problem for the Pandavas. The story is relevant even today.

1. It is said that in her earlier birth, Draupadi performed penance for the best husband. When she was asked to seek what she wanted, by the Mahadeva, she is said to have asked for five impossible traits in one husband. So, Mahadeva said that even for him it is not possible to create such an ideal person, but she would be married to five different persons who would have such characters. So, in the next birth, she was married to five men.

2. The second story involves the wives of Dharma, Vayu, Indra, and Ashwini Kumaras. For some reason, the Brahma cursed them that they all would be spending time on the earth as human forms. So, Shyamla (Dharma) Bharati, (Vayu) Shachi, (Indra), and Usha (Ashwini Kumar) descended to earth produced in a Yadnya, combined as Draupadi, and later on married their counterparts in

the earthly avatars.

3. In the third version, in her earlier birth, Draupadi was a very good-looking, and virtuous daughter of a rishi but somehow could not get married. So, to avoid the same fate in the next birth she did a great tapa and prayed to Mahadeva. When he appeared before her, she was very weak and her voice was even weaker. She asked for a husband and to make sure that the Mahadeva was listening properly she repeated her request five times. So, as a result in her next incarnation, as Draupadi, she was blessed with five husbands who were the best of the lots.

Now as in the cases of many other stories one has to either accept or find the logic. But one thing is sure all these stories are simply fantastic and very well narrated.

Shrikrishna was respectful towards Pandavas. Yudhishthira and Bhima were elder than him. Of them, he was closer to Bhima. For a dynamic person like Shrikrishna, the decisions of Yudhishthira could be inexplicable and unacceptable, but he never showed so. He was the same age as Arjun, so he was his *Sakha*, a friend. Nakul and Sahdev were younger, so they received love like younger siblings. It is not evident that any other person from the Yadav clan was close to Pandavas. Balram was more impressed by Duryodhana and he even thought about marrying his sister, Subhadra, to him. Others like Satyaki or Kritvarma were seemingly indifferent.

Why Shrikrishna was inclined to help is a question that has been answered by many, in many perspectives, but it seems that in the overall strategy devised by Shrikrishna of cleansing the earth of its wicked people, Pandavas fitted better. He found them *teachable* and probably more versatile than their cousins. The rest of the kings in the Bharatvarsha were not up to his scale of excellence.

Once the decision was taken, Shrikrishna moved at a speed only he could manage. He was already sure about the impending war. He knew that he would support the Pandavas. He knew the risks. Though the Pandavas were brave, they had their follies, they all had their attacks on the dharma and neeti. It is said that *the intelligent are full of doubts*, and Pandavas were not an exception.

One more thing we have to understand is about some people in India, want to glorify the villains. They do so only in Hindu contexts. They claim to be rational, but their rationality is selective, and it affects only Hindu epics. They glorify Ravana, Vali, Karna, Duryodhana, and all villains from different eras. They twist the contexts; they claim to be analytical and present the picture in a very prejudiced way so that the accepted heroes should look in a bad light. They would be scrutinizing the behaviour of the heroes like Ram, Laxman, Chanakya, Tulsidas, Shivaji, Sambhaji, Bajirao, Tilak, and Savarkar, and create an air of confusion. They would ridicule the Hindu ways of life, but conveniently forget all nonsense of their masters in China, Pakistan, America, and Middle Eastern countries. They want Hindus to forget that the Hindus are the only race that is the oldest and the best. Whatever anyone may say every other religion draws heavily from the Sanatan dharma.

(The Hindus over a period of ages have been very critical of the smallest mistakes committed by their heroes. Not only they are vocal, but they keep repeating the same for ages. When it is Ram, there is a set of mistakes, when there is Shrikrishna there is another set, they would try to tarnish the image. It continued right up to Veer Savarkar. The same type of information has been used very cleverly by the Christians and the Muslims for degrading the Sanatan dharma. And converting Indians to their faith. But very surprisingly, the same pseudo-liberals lot is very forgiving when they discuss the villains. They write books on Karna, Ravana, King Bali, and Vali the villain, and get recognized as the intellectuals. They get the fabricated awards which they later return when they cannot face the truth. ***A villain is a villain***. And secondly, none of these pseudo-intellectuals are anywhere near the capability of any great epic hero. So, what they say must be summarily ignored. They do not matter in the context of the Sanatan, as they have very little respect for the Indian culture, they see things wearing European or communist glasses. Their writings are loaded with a grudge, prejudice, and wrong education.

It is wrong to compare any two eras and find faults in those characters who cannot defend themselves. It is in vogue for Indians especially pseudo-seculars. There is a classic training probably given to these people to shoot wild accusations and then simply run away. Most of the recognitions showered upon these people come from NGOs outside India and against India. For the last two thousand years, a concerted and coordinated effort is on to undermine the Sanatan culture and dharma. Sadly, the foreigners are helped by a few half-baked Indians. Going one step further even if the Hindu epics are bad, they are not as *scientific* as western history (a big joke) but even then, why deride them? Who gives these people this right? The early Farsi and English- speaking Indian people in India have done the greatest damage to our culture. They tried to please their masters at the cost of Hindu esteem. They manipulated the facts, mixed them with contempt, and spread it across the world. Even today an average Indian does not know or does not care if he does not know about the history of Sanatan Bharat or the invaders. The only versions available depict the good side of their scant history recorded. We must teach the bloody history of the whites in Europe and America so that the polish of being sophisticated would be wiped off their faces.)

Whenever Shrikrishna was away the Pandavas always faced difficult times. It was neither by design nor by default. But somehow, they were saved by the smart thinking of Shrikrishna. There are many instances like the visit of Duravasa rishi with his thousands of disciples to the humble dwellings of Pandavas. Again, there was a certain involvement of their dear cousins. The worst incident was when the Pandavas crossed all limits of naivety and baited Draupadi against the loaded dice of Shakuni. That Yudhishthira would be losing the game was a foregone conclusion. He lost and then whatever happened was the worst moment in the life of all those who had some sense remaining in them. The Kauravas including the blind king Dhritrashtra, Karna, Ashwatthama, Duryodhana, and his brother Dusshasana were at the lowest ebb of human existence. Sadly, the elders were either not in a position to assert themselves or they chose to be silent. They were silent spectators when they should have stopped the fiasco. They did not. Shrikrishna was busy in the war with Shalva. And only the most intense call of Draupadi could make him aware of his need to protect the honour of a lady in distress caused by her own people. This particular chapter raises a lot of questions about the character of Dharmaraj and his following of the dharma. He was almost an egotist about following the dharma, and nothing else mattered. <u>Not even the honour of his wife</u>. It is difficult to understand why he did what he did, why his brothers obeyed him, and why the seniors allowed the dirtiest and most shameful incident to happen. Why the dharma allowed what was to happen? No explanations and citations from the dhramshastras would take away the pain of Draupadi or the insult of the Pandavas. The one-sided obeying of the dharma is questionable. (Sadly, it is happening even today. It is a great tribute to the Hindu population even today that they see that people like the politicians, police, judiciary, and many others profit, prosper, and become socially powerful, from doing the worst things and yet <u>they still follow the dharma</u>. The day the self-control of the common public goes off there would be chaos in our country.)

The prime requirement of the king is to win control over his mind. Vyas very clearly has said that the one, who cannot control his inner self, would never control the complex issues of the Rajya. Further, the entire onus of responsibility, for the fall in the values, the immoral behaviour of the Praja, and even for the crimes is entirely on the king. The king has to guard his treasury, ministry, judiciary, friends, and friend nations, and he can do so only when he can control his mind.

Mahabharata also raises a very valid question about the genesis of leadership.

The question is what comes first?

The circumstances or the leadership?

What generates what?

Present-day sociologists believe that the circumstances are responsible for begetting the leaders. For Mahabharata, it is the rules about circumstances that are responsible for the behaviour of the kings. The average king can be above average if he followed the guiding principles of the dhramshastras. It is so well-defined. The leadership was put to test only in exceptional circumstances and even then, the king had a very knowledgeable resource pool of the ministry. Probably because of the strength of these shastras Hindu kingdoms could sustain and survive the onslaughts of the invaders.

Mahabharata speaks clearly about the controls over the kingdoms apart from the king. The ministry, the purohits, the kulgurus, and the representatives from the gana or the blocks as in today's language had a major role to play in the smooth conduct of the kingdom. They saw to it that the king was not an imbecile, foolish, helpless, immature, womanizer, and without any other faults. At the same time, the king should be with knowledge, and pious, should act as per the shastra, be impartial, and with a strong network of friends and allies. (Please try to apply these conditions in our states, you would find very few who deserve to be on the chairs of a chief minister.)

So, before the advent of Shrikrishna in the Mahabharata, there was a set of rules, and a few exceptions but somehow the states were limping if not running. Mahabharat without Shrikrishna is unimaginable, but not vice versa. Mahabharat before Shrikrishna was bland like a dish without salt. What the salt does, adds the aspect of taste to the food. It makes it more palatable. The same thing happens to Mahabharat after Shrikrishna's entry. It becomes more interesting, more competitive, more responsive, and more like a well-conducted orchestra.

One story which reflects the great power and impact Shrikrishna had on the Mahabharat is about Arjun getting beaten by the tribal gang and his inability to protect the gopis he was supposed to deliver to Gokul.

The story is simple. Once Arjun visits Dwarka to see his friend Shrikrishna. As used to happen many times Narad appeared and told Arjun not to touch Shrikrishna as he was not well. There was no argument over what *Narad uvach*. When Shrikrishna sees Arjun, he asks him for a hug. Arjun says "no." Shrikrishna tells Arjun 'I feel very hurt. You are not coming anywhere near me; you are treating me indifferently. At least use your bow to scratch my wounds.' Arjun thought it to be okay. So, he obliges. Shrikrishna sucked the power from his bow. Then Shrikrishna asks Arjun to escort the gopis to the Gokul. While in the jungle the party was attacked by the tribal gang and Arjun could not do anything. He realizes that it was the end for him.

There is doha which describes the story in two lines.

तुलसी नर का क्या बडा़, **समय** बडा़ **बलवान** ।

भीलां लूटी गोपयिां ँ, वही अर्जुन वही बाण ॥

Without Shrikrishna the Mahabharat would be like a body without life.

The purpose of Shrikrishna's life in the second half was the re-establishment of the Dhramarajya like it was at the time of the Ram. But even for a divine person like Shrikrishna, it must be difficult. The reasons are the downfall in the moral values from Treta to Dwapar Yuga, the loose handling of the interpretations of the shastras, the arrogance of people like Jarasandha, Duryodhana, and the set of the people who knew which side is stronger and to please the same. Shrikrishna selected the Pandavas, not because they were the best suited to help him in his cause of the total annihilation of evil, but because they were more teachable. The policy of using the available resources was the guideline for Shrikrishna. He was aware of their follies, but he knew he could control and improve their performance. Shrikrishna could have done everything including the War, himself, without anyone to help, but that would have even more paralyzed the system. The dependence of the Praja on the god to sort out the problems would be more in the days to come. So, he assumed the role of a teacher, trainer, and motivator for the people he loved and made them win everything he wanted them to. As with anything else he surpassed all in doing so. He turned out to be the best friend, philosopher, and guide not only to Pandavas but to all of us several thousand years later.

***

Guidance for an Individual.

<u>Guidance for an Individual.</u>

When we study the Hindus, we have to fight many preconceived notions. There are many prejudices peddled and surprisingly these rumors or unsubstantiated facts have a stronger base than the facts. They are *there just like that* and with the passage of thousands of years, these *'facts'* are accepted. We have been brought up with the wrong facts, which seem very acceptable at least on the surface levels. Here the Hindus must understand the concept of *Maya*, which tries to hide the facts, as temporarily as the clouds hiding the sun for a while. In the interest shown by the Hindus, in their epics, Vedas, or Upanishads, and even the most fascinating Puranas, we find a very peculiar trend. There is a sense of fantasy more than their acceptance. There is a feeling that these books are just mythological and hence not to be given importance. The trend tells us that the Hindu youth ridicules without ever reading them. *However, the same Hindu students accept the facts in the books of other religious books.* They take it almost on the gospel truth level. The communist Hindus (if such a sample can exist) take pride in deriding them before disowning them. The family men simply do not have time for such trivial things. The ladies have a mixed reaction. One more trend tells us that it is conveniently understood that these oceans of knowledge are for the retired and old people. Such a waste of knowledge! They would never know the real meaning of life unless they read them. Sadly, even to know this simple fact they would have to study these epics.

We have to imagine the volume of concerted efforts on the part of the anti-Hindu gangs for over a period of two thousand years to dilute the wisdom of the Sanatan dharma. What is now accepted as truths coming from the United States or Russia, and to some extent from Germany were already known to a common Sanatan person. The level of knowledge of the saints and rishis was unfathomable. For example, the timing of the solar and lunar eclipses, the astronomical distances, and the atomic theories, they knew that the atom was divisible and they called it *anu, renu, or parmanu.* The point, which is to be underlined, is that because the knowledge was there and was distributed in a very clever manner to everyone as per his needs, the efforts of diluting and erasing the same are still on after two thousand years. Even now a billion people have survived the continuous onslaught. But now it seems that they have become even more precise in their operations. They are now destroying education, religion, demography, and the understanding of Sanatan dharma and sadly they seem to succeed. They are helped more by our not-so-own people.

Before any attempt to understand the Sanatan Dharma, the average Hindu person, who is at the receiving end from people who want to degrade the Sanatan Dharma, must know that the Sanatan dharma is the oldest living religion and it has taught the world that we can stay together, without any conflicts of interests. <u>No other religion has produced</u> so many distinguished men, writers, poets, dramatists, warriors, religion founders, sages by hundreds, innumerable saints, kings, gurus, statesmen, and millions of others in every walk of life. It is a religion that teaches to win without antagonizing the losers. Sanatan dharma followers never looted anyone, but always amicably settled the matters once the war was over. The eldest son of the conquered king was made the king. There was no killing of the male population, no rapes of the women and boys, like in the later part of the barbaric history.

No other religion has a better foundation than the Sanatan dharma. It is based on the superlative Dnyan given by the Creator to Manu and other brilliant rishis. The four Vedas, Upanishads, and the stories in the Puranas, the Ramayana, the Mahabharat, and the Bhagwat, all combine to provide solutions to all problems even in modern life. You should know that the present-day objections have been dealt with in the earlier days by way of debates and *shastartha*. Sanatan Dharma taught us *to respect* the questions and the label of being intolerant is the biggest joke thrust upon the Hindus by the invaders and looters.

No other religion can come anywhere near the Sanatan dharma in the aspects of structured education, neeti shastra, and the oldest languages. We are very unfortunate that we believed in the propaganda and forgot our treasure. We forgot that we have the best language in Sanskrit, now accepted as the most scientific and appropriate for computer programming.

The Hindus must remember that there is only **one supreme** existence, which is eternal, infinite, changeless, and formless. From it, we all arrive and to it, we all finally go. It can be like an ocean and we can be like a single wave, whatever the wave does it ultimately goes in the ocean only. It has no independent existence.

One more thing that a Hindu must understand is that probably no other religion has a concept of a *sukh*. There is no synonym for this word. Sukh includes the integration of happiness, contentment, pleasure, comfort, gratification, relief, luxury, delight, sunshine, rejoicing, and many such feelings.

The knowledge which is available in the epics is so vast and inclusive that any problem in the lives of a common Hindu would find solutions in these great creations. But the attitude of the Hindus is very timid and defensive. The dilution is more towards the north of river Narmada as compared to the southern parts of India. The reasons are many but one major reason that stands out is the proximity of the Mughals to these people. They still believe that the Mughals were the ones who improved the quality of the lives of the Hindus. The others believe that the British were benevolent and that India owes them a lot. They tell us that the British gave us mines, railways, hospitals, and even democracy. ***It is one of the most stupid arguments***. After independence, many pseudointellectuals think that they were better in the times of slavery. That is an ultimate tribute to their media management. Neither the Moghuls nor the British did anything in Bharat without any selfish intentions. That the government after independence was incompetent, with no vision, corrupt and partial to Muslims does not make the British good. Both were here with the single intention of looting and they did that very efficiently. On an absolute scale, we cannot blame them, after all, they were here for that purpose only. This is debatable and we should not waste our time on such activity, but at the same time, we must not be naïve to believe such nonsense.

One of my friends who is from Haridwar, working in BHEL, and a great philosopher used to tell us one fact. He said 'Look, people in hundreds of thousands come to Haridwar and Rishikesh for taking a holy dip in the Ganga. They come from far and with full faith. Does it mean *that everyone* in these cities *bathes* every day? No, many avoid taking a dip. What would you call them? Imbeciles, foolish or non-believers?' It was a bold and surprising statement, and we did not believe it. So, we checked with our friends in the other cities of Banaras, Prayagraj, Kanpur, and even Patna and we were surprised to know that it is a fact. Later on, we did some introspection. It is felt that there are many Hindus, who have so much by way of readymade knowledge at no extra cost, just like the free water of the Ganga flowing by them, who do not value their treasures. They refuse to believe in the epics, ask stupid questions and waste their lives. No other religion has so many people, who have no respect for their culture, traditions, religion, epics, or gods, and as a result, they distance themselves from their roots. They are neither with their own nor are acceptable to others, even if, when they convert.

Is there a proper time to know about the teachings of Yogeshwar Shrikrishna? Yes, there is! It is NOW.

Shrikrishna is an ocean of knowledge, wisdom, and practical intelligence. He is unfathomable, he is vaster than the universe. And why not? Is he not the one who created it?

Yet He lived a full life of a common man, leading the common, ignorant man and the Gyani man. He could communicate with both of them in a language easily understood by them.

Does he tell something useful for the common man? What a common man can learn from his charitra? Or is his knowledge exclusively for those who are learned and scholars? No, it is for all of us.

He tells Arjun in the Geeta that one should take that much water from the ocean of knowledge, which he can drink and satiate his thirst. It also tells that **the water from a small pond and a large lake serves the same purpose** and hence once you know the absolute truth you would automatically know the mystery of the complete Gyan. The shloka goes like this:

यावानर्थउदपानेसर्वतः समुप्लुतोदके।
तावान्सर्वेषुवेदेषुब्राह्मणस्यवजिानतः || 2/46||

A common example of a teaching class can explain in a simple way of the available knowledge and the capacity of the student. In any regular class, a teacher teaches all present in the class. His teachings are not available to the students who bunk the classes. Out of the ones who are present in the class, very few are attentive, they listen to the teacher (listen can be a combination of two words: list+ enumerate), others are just seating in the class, they hear at the most the sound of the teacher, so they remember the *noise*, not the words, so they do not get the meaning. What is to be noted is that the teacher does not give customized lectures. Very few students benefit, from the class while others just blame everything and everyone except themselves. Everyone has the inbuilt capacity to learn, but only a few are aware and ready to apply the same to achieve something extraordinary.

Similarly, Shrikrishna has told the best of teachings in Geeta, Mahabharat, and Uddahv Geeta. Wise people say that if we say Ramayana is the cultural *history* of the Bharatvarsha, then Mahabharata certainly would be the gigantic and comprehensive *encyclopaedia* of the cultural aspects of the Bharatvarsha. If the Ramayana, has dealt with details of the set of processes of the objectives of life and how to lead lives morally, Mahabharata gives some weightage to the shortcomings of a man, and despite the incompleteness of a common man it teaches how to set and accomplish the objectives. No matter what are the odds and whatever the opposition's strength, if you understand, trust and follow the teachings of Shrikrishna, in the end, you are bound to be successful. The last shloka in the Geeta, says:

यत्रयोगेश्वर:कृष्णोयत्रपार्थोधनुर्धर:।
तत्र श्रीर्वजियो भूतधिर्ध्रुवा नीतिर्मतिर्मम ॥ 18/78।

And means that wherever the god of yoga Shrikrishna and the ace archer (again there is a huge difference between being an archer and a *dhanurdhar*) Partha are present, there resides victory, prosperity, a stable mind, and morality. The superlatives in Sanskrit used in describing the greatness of Shrikrishna can never be translated into any other language.

Whatever it means is important but in actual life, it is the best key for anyone striving for success. One has to be as like as possible Arjun, prepare under the instructions of a guru as near as Shrikrishna, and you would be successful. It is not easy but is a better way than what we tend to follow. Our teacher told us the same thing so many times that we tend to think like them in tough situations, and it has somehow helped.

Shrikrishna is different from most gurus in the sense that others advised and returned to their duties. Not so Shrikrishna, he was with Arjun through thick and thin. He walked him through the entire war for eighteen days and nights. After the end of the day, Shrikrishna analyzed each day for the good and bad. He never slept before the tactics for the next day were worked out, after he received the inputs from his spy network. Shrikrishna not only taught, but like a true trainer, he waited and persisted until the student was ready to do what he taught. His instructions were clear and once the plan was finalized; he never tolerated any deviations. The only times he was held up somewhere else, and the Pandavas suffered huge losses. Like the killing of Abhimanyu, the decision of Bhima to let him enter the chakravyuh backfired. It further proved that Pandavas were very vulnerable in isolation.

So long as the Hindus have these divine epics, and they try to follow their teachings, there is nothing much left in the entire world that can be learned by the Hindus. Hindus must remember that they have the contents, and readymade solutions for the entire problems generated by the lesser mortals, and they are the only ones in the world who can reorganize and restructure the world order, they can clear the mess created by half-baked followers of the other *isms*. Only Hindus have the idea of *sattva, rajas, and the tamas* natures and their effect on the individual and the nation. One can use the information for his own sake and get closer to the ultimate destination or at least identify others who are not behaving as they should.

The Jeeva or the atman is not very concerned with the physical form. As soon as he is born, he is bound by the triad of the gunas. He goes through pleasure or trauma and he behaves like an ordinary mortal controlled by the triguna.

Persons who follow the sattva gun *tendency* would be contented, at peace, and help. They do things that are good for everyone. They are self-radiant and quite knowledgeable. So, they have best the best chance to be with Yogeshwar Shrikrishna forever. But this does not always happen, they are transferred to the tamas *gun* because of the *ahankara* they develop. The three Gunas are quite interchangeable and the persons are moving through the mixture of the three or at their purest form.

The people who follow the rajogun, *rajas tendency* have been very common. They are just like you and me. They like to be with a wife, family, and children. They put a lot of effort into maintaining their worldly status. Modern men, across the world, are controlled by the objectives and achieving them in any which way possible. In the triad of gunas, they still are better than the tamasic gun people. And in absolute terms, if the best of the lot the sattva guni people have a limited chance of permanent salvation, the other two should think for themselves.

Ignorant people are generally very prone to commit mistakes, they can be lazy and the worst is that they love their sleep. This sleep can be of the physical form as well as the spiritual form.

In the 9/14 chapter of the Geeta, Shrikrishna clearly says that the sattva gun binds the man with such, the rajas gun binds the man with karma along with expectations (sakam-karma) and the tamo-guna covers whatever knowledge he has, and binds the person with stupidity.

The point to be noted is that these three are dominant or submissive in all living forms and they are interchangeable. The fact is like a two-edged sword. One can be transformed for better or worse depending upon his choice of karma.

There is a story of a mango tree that explains the concept. How each person each tendency responds to a simple tree gives clear insight. Story goes like

In a village, there lived three friends. For the sake of understanding, we would call them as sat, raj and timir. In the usual cycle of famine, they decide to quit their village and go to the bigger town for earning a livelihood. They walk a long distance before they decide to rest. Their tiffins were already exhausted and they had nothing to eat. What they do then is the story.

Sat finds a mango tree. He thanks God, and proceeds for picking some mangoes. But just before he was about to pluck the mangoes off the tree, he sees a good number of ripened mangoes fallen on the ground. He chooses from them and eats them. His hunger and thirst were taken care of. As a return of favor, he selects some big seeds and buries them thinking that some more trees would be useful in the future. He comes back and praises the taste and quality of the mangoes.

The raj goes next. He does quite similar to what his friend had done. But he thinks that he should collect some more mangoes which he could sell in the town. So, he cuts a large branch and puts a lot of mangoes in his bag. He goes back and brags about his smartness.

After the two the last one the tamas goes to the tree. He saw the tree in its full glory. Instead of being happy he recalled that he had planted seeds in his childhood but none became a tree. He was jealous. He was angry. He wanted to destroy the tree for no real reason. He plucked a sour mango. It was a green mango. Tamas did not have even basic common sense about a ripe and raw mango. When he ate a sour mango, his anger multiplied many times. He concluded that the two friends had all sweet ones. He was livid and he took out a matchbox and set the tree on fire. He destroyed what was not his.

Can you relate with the people around you? Throughout your active lives, you would be meeting one of the three characters. Try to understand why they behave the way they do and you would be quite happy.

***

But the Hindus should take a call on whom they should include and whom they should not. To expect others to be as enlightened as the Hindus is the stupidity that has caused us the maximum damage and we still suffer from that complex. People who are of a less calibre would always pull you down and that is what exactly happens with the Sanatan dharma. When you know you cannot reach someone's higher level best way is to pull him down. They would provoke incite, and ridicule, and would want that you should stoop down to their levels. That is what has been done with the Indians from outside and from inside for the last two hundred years. Again, the insiders are more dangerous, so the Hindus must have a standard operating procedure to negate their impact on the already sagging morale of the Hindus. The hurt inflicted by the close ones and insiders is ten times more intense than the outsiders. It hurts in two ways, the physical one is less painful while the other one is with the hurt of betrayal also. Bharatvarsha was never beaten by outsiders unless helped by the insiders. The tragedy is that we still seem to not learn this simple fact. We forgive the traitors, who should be condemned and never included in the process of nation-building.

Shrikrishna was a man of process and systems. He was always doing something, however trifle it seemed which would take him to his objectives in life. He said after accomplishing the primary objective of the Kamsa Vadha, that he needs to concentrate on the Karya of *dharma sansthapanayarth*, meaning the re-establishment of the Sanatan dharma and take it back to the level of what it was in the Ram Rajya in the earlier Tretayug.

Shrikrishna had a pre-decided role for his avatar. There was nobody who could direct him as he was the only one who knew what is to be done. Many stories are prevalently kept running by the kathakars who do a fantastic job of preserving the ethos of Sanatan dharma. But they take a lot of liberties and use exaggerations than the truth. Though their intentions are not wicked, they make things larger than life. But we cannot say so in the cases of some foreign authors and self-proclaimed Indologists. They have a terrible vested interest and they present a spoilt and wicked picture of the Hindu epics. As if they are not enough, we have a band of Indian pseudointellectuals who do their part in maligning the epics and the history. None of these may have faith systems in place. The bastardized education system intentionally forced on the gullible Indians during the British rule has created an army of anti-Indian, half-baked, and pseudo-seculars who have for the past two hundred years tried wholeheartedly to spoil the Indian ethos across the world. Sadly, they have more than moderately succeeded.

<u>The worst attack on any country is on its value systems</u>. Continuous defective malware is put inside the brains of students for over two thousand years. People from the "advanced" social groups like the Brahmo Samaj, never really understood that they were cleverly used by the British. They may have done some good things but their major contribution was in demeaning the traditions of the Hindus. If they wanted to improve the lots then they should have followed the methods used by Chaitanya Mahaprabhu, or swami Vivekananda. We have to achieve the zero level first to further achieve anything worthwhile. Running away from your religion to improve it, is like working overtime in your dream.

When you get up in the morning everything is the same as it was. Sometimes it may be even worse. You have to improve the dharma then you have to have the knowledge and a deep trust in the value systems. People of such groups and all those who converted to some other faiths have helped all those from the outside world in destroying the Sanatan dharma. We have to fight these dangerous weeds even more intensely now if we have to survive.

If one has to understand what Shrikrishna wants us to do to re-establish the Sanatan dharma we have to start learning Sanskrit first. An example is worth coating here. Israel and India became independent practically at the same time. India has been talking of diversity, but it is restricted to states within a country, and we are struggling to decide even on the national language. In the case of Israel, the people who are less than ten million came to their promised land from approximately one hundred and fifty countries. They have revived their two thousand years old Hebrew and use it now as their language for communication and everything else. We have probably made the biggest blunder by falling prey to false propaganda by the leftists by debasing Sanskrit from the curriculum and even worse from the minds of Hindus.

There is one doubt lurking in the minds of the Hindu youth about the relevance of the knowledge in Vedas, Upanishads, and epics like Ramayana and Mahabharata. There has been no effort on purpose to clean this clutter from the minds. The rest of the world considers India as a mere but the biggest market and as a country with a maximum number of young people who should be mentally corrupted. The efforts to do so are subtle and very effective.

In any other country the usage of foreign goods (due to the craze created by slavery and now the media,) foreign principles, foreign food, and foreign entertainment is not as bad as it is in India. The maximum youth in India in their own words is zapped by foreign influence which is hollow and materialistic. The sooner the Indian youth understands this trap the better would be his chances to rule the world. No other nation except India has accepted foreign goods, religions, cuisine, dressing, divorce, and abortions, as easily and on a mass scale as the Indians. Even their name Indian is a rootless entity enforced by the intellectually inferior people who could not pronounce our names. Nobody is bothered. We have behaved just like the Pandav king Dharmaraj, who gave away everything his own and which was not his own. He lived a life that had a lot of unanswered questions. We also have many.

Shrikrishna has always said the decisions you take in life are personal. He says that the elements which govern decision-making are personal. Every new aspiring manager must read Geeta as it is more likely to teach management than any modern greats like Kotler or Drucker. Geeta discusses in detail the management, but it is slightly more disguised. Your understanding would be better after reading and re-reading.

Shrikrishna has given stressed the correct estimating of a project or a problem. He demonstrated it amply in his life that one has to gather information, analyze, decide the best course of action, and then very importantly execute the plan. Karma yoga is a complex subject but in simple words, it glorifies the value of doing something rather than thinking about the negatives. Shrikrishna also helps you, young people, to get rid of the fear of failure, Shrikrishna says you do *the best* that you can, but it is imperative that you give your best effort and then leave the results to him. It is not easy in the era of instant gratification, but young people would have to learn if they have to succeed. They have to learn to be more innovative and productive so that they become powerful in the eyes of the people around them.

One more important thing he said was about having absolute integrity. The confusion, in the minds of Dronacharya, Bhishma, and many others, who fought against the just cause of the Pandavas, is very similar to the people who are doing the same error in modern India. No person is larger than the nation, but most political parties have forgotten the importance of this tenet. In present-day India, very few care for national interests. The national interest is a matter of ridicule and the pseudo-intellectuals have even coined the term hyper-nationalist. If one talks about the nation or the Hindus he is immediately branded as a hyper-nationalist. Shrikrishna has clearly said that nobody is larger than the dharma or the Bharatvarsha. While talking to Arjun just before the war he said that if anyone has any doubtful intention toward the Bharatvarsha, he must be eliminated. One wrong person tends to grow fast and create a fleet of anti-nationals.

Shrikrishna has said a few things which are very important for any individual. The summary could be:

- The first thing you have to understand is what matters is *you*.
- The problems are *yours* and you alone are *responsible* for finding the solutions.
- Listen carefully to everyone.
- Avoid pre-mature judgments.
- Even a third-grade ordinary person can give you a first-class idea that can change your life.
- Your intelligence does not always help you in life. You have to depend upon many factors to achieve something spectacular.
- Ask for help, you would be surprised to know that people are happy to help you.
- You would need people around you to enjoy your success.
- Read, learn, practice, and then preach.
- Success is a process that begins by defining your idea of success. You must have a crystal-clear idea.
- Learn to respect the mind. You have your exclusive mind a sub-mind and a subconscious mind.
- If you cannot re-condition your mind who else can do it for you? Others cannot help you.

Shrikrishna was a great motivator. He motivates even today, with his teachings in the Geeta and many have acknowledged the impact of Geeta on their success. No other book in the history of mankind has been read, written about, discussed, blogged, picturized, and preached for the betterment of individuals. It is not for conversion.

The common people must understand that the ancient Vedic philosophy of the Sanatan dharma was so popular in almost all civilized countries during that time, it spread without any canvassing. There was no force. The logic was impeccable and yet today the country where it originated finds that there is a concerted effort to denigrate it. Shrikrishna tells us about the power of Sangh, fraternalism. Roughly put it is feelings or emotions in the mind of one person for the other person. In a group, every individual has a personal goal or ambition. At least, it is the prerequisite for being a rational human being. Once it is accepted the understanding of interdependence comes to the fore. However good a human being is he has to depend on others for a few things in his life. It not only helps to accomplish goals but also helps in a generation of new ideas which seemed impossible before you met the person and interacted. A small push or casual correction can lead to great success.

The association, staying together, growing together, enjoying together, working together towards a common goal, and while doing so exchanging ideas some useful others not so can make a group, a religion very acceptable. In absence of interaction and exchange of ideas the activity in whatever form would be short-lived. Shrikrishna promoted bilateral communication but reserved the right of decision to himself.

Shrikrishna tells us about how a king should be in a very straightforward way. The king if he follows the actual raj dharma, should treat his Praja like a loving father, he should protect the weak and should generate taxes only for the public welfare, and development. He must set aside the evil people, isolate them, and eliminate them by either putting them in the prison or asking them to leave the country.

Shrikrishna not only tells us how each section of the society should behave in the larger interest of the nation. He differentiates between the *brahmasum* and the *devosum* brahmins. He tells us so many things in so many details that we wonder whether we needed a constitution based on the British version. The various systems called *pranali (systems)* are the real guidelines for a society that wants to be superior in all aspects. He also describes the division of society strictly based on **karma and never based on birth.**

He explains the importance of the fines (*dand*) in the overall administration of the State. He even describes the effect on a state where there is no able king. The diagnostic features of anarchy are the oppression of the weak, conversion of fellow humans into slaves, the extorsion, the forceful abduction of the ladies and raping them, infighting over the differences of the ways of worshipping, moral, ethical, and monetary corruption and the big fish consuming the small fish and such things which are very obvious. Such states invite the rule of the invaders as there are many offended, hurt, and insulted people, who are on the lookout for possible allies to combine with and topple the existing anarchy. What the Indians right from Ambhi, Jaichand, Malik Ghafoor, More, Suryaji Pisal, Mir Jaffar, to the recent versions of the traitors in the Lutyens Delhi, who are siding with the enemy states, religions and ideologies *forget* is that they are just a useless piece of information for an enemy who uses them like a tissue paper. They throw them as soon as their use is over. There is nothing new that is happening now, it is just a repeat telecast of many incidents from history. The sad and infuriating part is we never seem to learn from our history.

The description of the political and societal systems in the Bharatvarsha is so unique and well before the Greek, Roman, or Chinese philosophies. The ancient Hindu social scientists believed that the samaj-purush is the manifestation of the Supreme. That there is a cycle (just like the product life cycle in modern management where there is inception, growth, saturation, and decline of a product) that involves the journey of society from the rise to ruins and once again to the rise with some changes. When society is at the top of the moral and ethical ladder some indulge in materialistic pleasures while other enlightened ones engage in the further development of the self and the society. The first types cause the downfall of the society by doing all described in the diagnostic features of anarchy while the latter type strengthens the basic core of the society. That the Bharatvarsha could sustain the continuous attacks on its physical and philosophical assets is a tribute to the teachings of such people. After so many hundreds of years of tyranny, torture, anarchy, invasions, and conversions if the Sanatan dharma still is alive then we have to thank the people in the enlightened category who imbibed on the minds of the common people what to believe in, and whom to discard. The common Hindu man is slightly shy, who is weak in expression but is very clear about the value systems of the Sanatan dharma. They have their ways of discerning and deciphering the misinformation piled on them for centuries. Now is the time when probably their silent contribution would be vindicated and maybe the Sanatan society would once again be at the top of the development cycle.

The cause and the process of the re-establishment of the Sanatan dharma is not a job of a single person, but it would have to involve the entire population. The process would be three-pronged. Establishing the correct facts, wiping out the wicked propaganda, and the correct practice of the Sanatan dharma without the karmakanda.

***

Shrikrishna, As the Saviour.

Shrikrishna, As the Saviour.

What would you do if you are lost in a complex maze, where you do not find a way out? You try all possible lanes and yet you would reach nowhere. Maybe by fluke, you would get out, but the chances are very less. Moreover, if the maze is like a game, you know that there would be at least *sure* that there would be some way out and it is just a matter of time before you would be relieved of the tension. But the maze called *life* has different challenges. In the real life, there is *no* guarantee that there would be a solution to your problems. And the worst part is that you understand this irony only at the end of your life. You may struggle, you may put in all your best efforts, and yet you would fail. What you do, *then would* decide whether you are really *up to* it or you would end up in the *also-ran* category of the world. There are challenges thrown at you by the people, and destiny, and they bank upon your inability to solve the issues. They would further wait for you to fail so that they could say that they already knew it. In such a situation whom would you approach? Would you approach a person who reminds you of your mistakes? Or would you approach the one who accepts you with your mistakes, consoles you, comforts you, and tells you 'Do not worry, we would find a solution to your problem. You are not the only one who has faced this problem and they are relieved, so relax and let us find out the way.'

The basic purpose of the eighth avatar was to save the good people from the bad, cruel, immoral oppressors.

In his entire life, Shrikrishna has *never ridiculed* a person when he approached him (Shrikrishna) with a problem. He with his magnetic smile accepted the person as he was and offered him the best possible solution. Whether it was the case of residents of Gokul, the oppressed people of Mathura, or his friend Sudama, or Draupadi in her distress, Shrikrishna always _helped_ first. Shrikrishna knew that the person wants comfort firstly and secondly a solution to his problem and not the usual Gyan meted out by people to the person in distress.

Once, a clerk in the Mumbai office loses his salary on the first of the month, as his wallet was picked in a local train. The next day he goes to the office early in the false hope that he might have forgotten the wallet in his drawer. While he was checking everybody laughed at him, poked fun at him, ridiculed him, and told him so many things, but nobody helped him. He became a subject of entertainment for a while and he could not answer back as he was in shock. At last, after the end of the usual nonsense, he was seating at his desk crestfallen, trying to figure out how to cope with the monthly requirements, one most unexpected person approaches him. The person was never taken seriously by anyone in the office, including by the one who lost his wallet. The person gives his pay packet to the clerk and says **nothing else can replace the pay packet**, except money. The clerk was overwhelmed and just shook his hands and gives a smile in gratitude. No words were needed.

So, when someone is in distress either help him or console him as a second choice, but never tell him, at least in the beginning, where did he go wrong. He knows that he has made a mistake, he is already brooding over the same, he is sulking, and he is unhappy so why increase his discomfort by telling him unnecessary things? Shrikrishna did the same and extended his help. Shrikrishna helped everyone without compromising the dignity of the person in distress. So even today when a sensible person is facing uneasy times, due to a quirk of fate or his folly he finds a soothing solace in the words of Shrikrishna. He can find a way to solve his problems. He understands that none of his problems can be so huge that they would not be solved using the wisdom available in the Geeta or the Mahabharata.

The first step is the easiest for the persons who follow the *bhakitiyog* which needs a complete surrender to the mystical powers of Shrikrishna. When the bhakta offers his complete self with his egos, problems, expectations, and inability to cope with the wicked world, he is accepted by Shrikrishna with open arms and a ready-to-help smile. Subsequently, nothing else matters. He is taken care of and he is left with only one job which is to do the bhakti. Right from the times when Shrikrishna was here to the present day many people have experienced the omnipotent and omnipresent Shrikrishna and their lives have been blessed. They do not need anything else anymore.

But for those who are intellectuals, at least they think they are, it is very difficult for them to surrender. They start by questioning the very presence of Yogeshwar Shrikrishna. Their limited intelligence finds it beyond its scope to understand the vastness of Shrikrishna. They even have promoted the concept of multiple Shrikrishna *instead of one* as they feel that one person **cannot accomplish** so much. Same thing they say about Maharshi Vyas. The basic problem of these people is that they revere some tin-pots in the present day of pseudo-hypes, who have climbed the materialistic ladders in any which way possible, mostly immoral. People like Lenin, and later Stalin rose to become the leaders of the shortest living *ism* called communism to become leaders, pale in comparison, when compared with Shrikrishna, Buddha, or Jesus Christ. One of the most dangerous things the Indian communists started in the early fifties of the last century was the inception of the society of atheists and through which they presented a very perverse picture of the Hindu gods, Hindu history, Hindu culture, Hindu traditions, and even the prime language Sanskrit. They had a free field as the then government also wanted the same. Communists never touched

Islam as they were in mortal fear of life. They concentrated mainly on denigrating the Krishna, Ram, and Hindu epics. The lopsided intelligence of people like S.A. Dange is very obvious, in a propagandist book named 'From primitive communism to slavery' he used the technique, later perfected by the pseudointellectuals at the JNU and such anti-national institutes and the gazetted and paid history writers of saying anything illogical and never prove. Mr. Dange just questioned everything and answered nothing. He followed people like Moriz Winternitz, a colleague of Max Muller at Oxford University. Therefore, the intelligence of such people and their remarks are to be taken with a pinch of salt. The purity of intention of the pure research is at stake as they were inclined and loaded with partiality towards European superiority and Christianity. They were doing a duty towards their countries, but what people like Dange achieved by showing Hindu culture in poor light is a matter of research. As a founder member of the now almost dead communist party in India, Dange damaged the interest of the Sanatan dharma to an unreasonable limit. He tries to nullify the research done by so many like Lokmanya Tilak, Rajwade, Bhandarkar, and Jaiswal, without any worthwhile logic or data. There was a generation of such people who were in the category of brown sahib, who behaved most irresponsibly and tried to defame anything good in the Hindu culture. Now if you see that the birthplace of communism Russia claims to be a Christian country. Even the book Discovery of India should fall in the same category of defaming rather than the historical account of India. That they succeeded in simply wiping out one thousand years of history is a credit to their organized effort.

The "I feel so, hence" types of comments by many in India and abroad, on the Sanatan dharma must be dismissed summarily. Dr. Bhandarkar, Shri. Chintaman Vaidya and many have tried to explain their views in a very haphazard way. They should have used their intelligence in the Karya of *dharma sansthapanayarth* instead of trying to unnecessarily destroy the value systems. Their claims of multiple Shrikrishna, and their views on the behaviour of the characters like Shayla, Dronacharya, Bhishma, and Ashwatthama, need to be tackled dispassionately.

To understand what Shrikrishna is, one has to have some Hindu DNA. Otherwise, it is very difficult to comprehend. European and American scholars have studied Indian culture, but they study Indology, without absorbing the Indian ethos. They approach with doubt and apprehension. They take simple Hindus for simpletons. They cannot somehow accept that the **Hindus were and are better than them.** They try to undermine the ancient importance and influence of Hindu dominance over the entire known world at that time. Their style is simple. They raise doubt and leave it there. They pinpoint the negatives if any.

So, to know what is wrong and what is right, we Hindus, have to first know what is in the Mahabharata, and the Geeta. We as Indians **must read the epics** in any of our languages. We must know the opulence, the richness of the creations which no other country has. In one of the shlokas of Adi Parva, it is said "yadi hasti tadnyatra, yannehasti na tat kwachit" which when translated means that which exists in the Mahabharata exists everywhere in the world, and what is not in Mahabharata does not exist anywhere in the world. It is not an exaggeration but truth, it includes not only the great war of Kauravas and Pandavas, but it gives a comprehensive account of the Aryan philosophy, theology, history, political science, moral science, and organizational behaviour science. The epic is called the encyclopaedia of Sanatan dharma and also the fifth Veda.

The point to be noted by all nationalist Hindus is before accepting any negative comments from any acknowledged intellectuals or pseudo-intellectuals, they must verify the intent with which it is written. Not everything that is written by foreigners is with the purest of intentions. There are many factors and compulsions which regulate the intellectuals and their conscience. People who wrote Indian history were sadly not Indians. They were either foreigners or Indians who had sold their souls to the British or the Congress party. So, whatever they have written needs to be seriously reviewed. The Hindus have to redefine the concept of intolerance. While the Sanatan dharma is probably the only tolerant religious philosophy existing in the world, it is constantly under the attack of communists, pseudo-seculars, Islamists, and others who see Hindus as the most easily converted by people in the world.

Coming back to the role as a saviour, Shrikrishna enjoyed the unique faith and trust of those who were close to him. They may not have known him for long, but they had implicit faith in his capacity. After the Draupadi swayamvaram, they were discussing whether or not the Pandavas should go to Hastinapur or not, the father of the bride king Drupad said that Shrikrishna cares for the Yudhishthira and his brothers much more than anybody else in the world. And the Pandavas must listen to his advice in the future. The shloka in the Adi parva says "न तद ध्यायती कौंतेय: पांडूपुत्रो यध्रष्ठि्ठरि: यथैषां पुरुष व्याघ्र श्ररेया ध्यायति केशव:"

Another clear-cut indication of the Pandavas considering Shrikrishna as their sole saviour becomes obvious when Yudhishthira, despite all advice and promises from many, could not decide whether he should go for the big event of the Rajsuya Yadnya. He sent an urgent invitation to Shrikrishna and when they met Yudhishthira very plainly and humbly asked for formal permission from Shrikrishna. He said 'O Vasudev unless you approve that I am worthy of conducting the Rajsuya I would not go for it. Many tell me that I should go ahead, but I am not sure about their intentions and sincerity toward me. I know that unless you tell me to proceed, I would not even think of it. The Rajsuya would be successful only when each king accepts me as the Chakravarty Samrat. You are the only one who has no evil thoughts for us, you always wish the Kalyan for us, so, please tell me what to do.'

Further when Shrikrishna asked for the two brothers Arjun and Bhima, to go and defeat the Jarasandha Yudhishthira was very pleased and said 'Now I am sure that Jarasandha would be finished, the kings in his captivity would be liberated, and our Rajsuya would be successful. You are the foremost among us. We are your followers. You are our only saviour, and we are grateful for this blessing. I know that once you are with us, we would be prosperous, and victorious, and we assure you that we would be in your command henceforth.' He followed his promise and the only time he spoke the half-truth about the killing of the Ashwatthama the elephant, was also under the instructions of Shrikrishna.

Just before the war when Arjun opted for Shrikrishna and not his *invincible* army, the Narayanisena again shows that Shrikrishna was accepted by them as their sole saviour. This could be the one singular act of wisdom that helped the Pandavas ultimately win the war. Arjun was sure that the side which had Shrikrishna was decided to win, whether he had his shastra, Astra, and whether he fought or not. How can Shrikrishna the saviour of the universe can lose? His confidence paid off, and he was blessed with a historic win.

His presence is felt in everything of the Mahabharat, just like we the believers feel his presence today. There are instances in the lives of people like Saint Dnyaneshwar, Tukaram, Ramdas, Eknath, Kabir, and Meerabai, who have described their merging with Shrikrishna. In the last century, one of the most intellectual persons Maharshi Aurobindo has described his experience. It goes like this *"I looked at the jail that secluded me from men and it was no longer by its high walls that I was imprisoned; no, it was Vasudeva who surrounded me. I walked under the branches of the tree in front of my cell, but it was not the tree, I knew it was Vasudeva, it was Sri Krishna whom I saw standing there and holding over me his shade. I looked at the bars of my cell, the very grating that did duty for a door and again I saw Vasudeva. It was Narayana who was guarding and standing sentry over me. Or I lay on the coarse blankets that were given me for a couch and felt the arms of Sri Krishna around me, the arms of my Friend and Lover. This was the first use of the deeper vision He gave me. I looked at the prisoners in the jail, the thieves, the murderers, the swindlers, and as I looked at them, I saw Vasudeva, it was Narayana whom I found in these darkened souls and misused bodies."* (Realization in Jail Savitri)

If you feel his presence around you, please be rest assured that you are the blessed one. If you have faith in him your life would be easy. You would be free of the responsibility of karma. He takes over your life.

But there is a small precondition, that you have *to perform* your daily duties in the best possible ways.

As for those who deny the existence of the supreme power in any form, especially Shrikrishna there is a small thought that they should ponder upon. When there is a denial of God then the only argument rests on the inner voice of the mind. They forget that the mind is the manifestation of the entire influx of the thoughts, teachings, reading, and listening of the wisdom coming from the elders. They also forget that the concept of mind is in itself a believer's thought. The existence of the mind is also a matter of assumption. It is not to be seen, but the power is inescapable. The mind is the closest to the atman or the souls and not to the body. So, when the bodies are physically similar, in all mankind except maybe in colour etc why do some humans distinguish themselves? They do it based on their power of the mind, the power they are blessed with by the supreme power.

Again, if the discerning power of the mind is to be equated with the supreme power, we have to understand the basic difference. In the cases of those non-believers who spend a major part of their lives gathering the data, checking its relevance, then analyzing it, then getting confused, and finally may be in taking wrong decisions. But in the case of the believers, he gets strength from the automatic power emanating from the belief in their Shrikrishna. They do not waste time in data management as they get it ready-made. They know that if they do their daily duties in the best possible ways the rest is taken care of by saviour Shrikrishna. Life of these people become simple. For example, the super network of the dabbawallas in Mumbai. What they have been doing for decades without any formal education is best explained by their belief in the Vitthala, again a roopam of the Shrikrishna. Their control is in the form of a necklace they wear. It is called a *mala* and these people are called the *malkarees, who wear the mala.* There is a near cent-percent efficiency index in their operation which has very little need of formal supervision or control for so many years in which Mumbai city has grown from a city to a huge metropolis. How they have coped with the changing scenario is a topic of research. But for the Shrikrishna Bhaktagan, the only thing that helps them through all their difficulties is their implicit faith in their deity the Vitthala.

What does a saviour do in these times? What are the expectations? Does he come to you or he sends some signals? Who approaches whom? Does he need any approach? Or is he just a call away? How many times he can be called? Is it like, some magic that needs a code or password? What are the types of problems he can save you from? Is the best option or there is someone else? If you think that you would be as it is *saved* so you have a license to go on doing wrong things or mistakes?

These are some of the questions young people have today. They know a little bit of everything, and they try to interpret as per their understanding or lack of it. The basic thing they tend to forget is that there are no conditions in the bhakti. It is a faith-based process and a no-questions-asked approach to the Yogeshwar Shrikrishna. He may or may not help you and it is expected of you to be happy in both cases. It is not an instant gratification process. He would probably test you and your intentions before he helps you. He has his logic and his own set of rules and he decides as per his standards, whether you are worth it or not. He is the only god who is having a very practical and sensible approach toward everything.

Before asking to be rescued or saved by him one has to understand the meaning of the word blessing or Ashirwad. If you are blessed it never means that you would bet everything served on the proverbial platter. Whether blessed or not you still have the same duties, but when you are under the kripachhtra, an umbrella of his blessings, you enjoy whatever comes your way. You become nonchalant or the sthitpragya and wait for the bad times to pass. You double your efforts for the ultimate aim of merging with the Vasudev Swaroopa. When the feeling of dukh is taken away whatever remains is the Sukh.

The saviour himself prefers the people who follow the Bhakti Marg. One has to understand that attaining the swarga is not the same as merging fully with Shrikrishna. The swarglok pales in comparison when compared to the Vishnu Lok or the ultimate destination of Vaikuntha. The sweet description of Shrikrishna is best in the Madhurashtakam, it is so apt that each devotee would feel blessed even if he just recites it. It is one of the sweetest tributes to the almighty Shrikrishna.

मधुराष्टकम्

madhurashtakam

अधरं मधुरं वदनं मधुरं
नयनं मधुरं हसितं मधुरम् ।
हृदयं मधुरं गमनं मधुरं
मधुराधिपतेरखिलं मधुरम् ॥ 1 ॥

वचनं मधुरं चरितं मधुरं
वसनं मधुरं वलितं मधुरम् ।
चलितं मधुरं भ्रमितं मधुरं
मधुराधिपतेरखिलं मधुरम् ॥ 2 ॥

वेणुर्मधुरो रेणुर्मधुरः
पाणिर्मधुरः पादौ मधुरौ ।
नृत्यं मधुरं सख्यं मधुरं
मधुराधिपतेरखिलं मधुरम् ॥ 3 ॥

गीतं मधुरं पीतं मधुरं
भुक्तं मधुरं सुप्तं मधुरम् ।
रूपं मधुरं तिलकं मधुरं
मधुराधिपतेरखिलं मधुरम् ॥ 4 ॥

करणं मधुरं तरणं मधुरं
हरणं मधुरं रमणं मधुरम् ।
वमितं मधुरं शमितं मधुरं
मधुराधिपतेरखिलं मधुरम् ॥ 5 ॥

गुञ्जा मधुरा माला मधुरा
यमुना मधुरा वीची मधुरा ।
सलिलं मधुरं कमलं मधुरं
मधुराधिपतेरखिलं मधुरम् ॥ 6 ॥

गोपी मधुरा लीला मधुरा
यक्तं मधुरं मुक्तं मधुरम् ।
दृष्टं मधुरं शष्टिं मधुरं
मधुराधपितरेखलिं मधुरम् ॥ 7 ॥
गोपा मधुरा गावो मधुरा
यष्टरिमधुरा सृष्टरिमधुरा ।
दलति मधुरं फलति मधुरं
मधुराधपितरेखलिं मधुरम् ॥

वल्लभाचार्य (Vallabh Acharya.)

When you accept Shrikrishna as your guru, mentor, Sakha, and ultimate destination you are right on the path to salvation. When you feel that you do not exist as a separate entity, but you are a part (ansha) of the Divya Swaroopa of the Yogeshwar Shrikrishna, you have attained the final salvation.

What you are, does not matter. What you do does not matter. Nothing else then matters!

***

CHAPTER ELEVEN

Shrikrishna: As a Manager

Shrikrishna: As a Manager

Modern management systems, started somewhere in the third decade of the twentieth century, due to the urgent need for engineers to understand and apply the commercial aspects of the business. Modern management systems are more like a review and compilation of already-known facts. People like Peter Drucker did a systematic cataloguing of the proposed process and its expected benefits. He did a great job.

What is however forgotten in the hyping of modern management is that business had earlier flourished in the ancient world. People in the continents were privy to their hard-earned knowledge and data. They had their systems, controls, leadership, and decision-making. Surprisingly the systems varied from the community, region, and nation. They were tried and tested for centuries, customized for the various needs of the customers and the knowledge was passed to the next generations by the elders. The refinement was there due to excessive scrutiny and a huge sample for each business. In Bharatvarsha, the Hindus were masters in silk manufacturing, metallurgy, weaponry, animal husbandry, dairy farming, civil engineering, food, and in so many other things, which were not even heard of during that time in the rest of the world. Bharat was ruling the world in commercial and international trade. We still do not know much about the process where two traders conducted a deal under the handkerchief, using their fingers. They did not talk, and they conducted business right in the middle of the crowded market. Apart from those two nobodies knew about the rates, the quantities, deliveries, and anything else. Their method was fool proof and it lasted for centuries.

Hindus were also leading in philosophical and scientific matters. The Hindus should be proud of their forefathers and the way they ruled the world without any force or coercion. They did not poach on anybody else's business. They were happy doing their things for generations. Now we are forced to forego what we knew, and we now hardly know the way international business is conducted. The ruthlessness, the disregard for entrepreneurship, the takeover culture, the questionable ethics, the business espionage, the hyper impact on the spread of business, money earned *in any which* way possible, and many such things have made all businesses more of a war than a simple exchange of goods and services. Nobody seems to be secure; nobody has any sense of belonging. One major difference in the domination of the world by us the Sanatan and the present-day materialistic hollow people is we were in sync with nature. We were holistic and conservative, we believed in organic methods, and we were not wanting to change other people, their culture, and their way of worship. And yet the entire planet which mattered followed the Sanatan way of life without distancing them from their way of life. In the last five hundred years, the so-called advanced people have exploited and ruined the basic balance of the planet. Maybe, they have some accomplishments here and there, but they pale in the light of the permanent destruction they have caused.

One of the prime exponents of Sanatan management was Shrikrishna. He was a master of achieving results with available resources. He won where his chances of winning were very negligible. He defeated Kamsa, Jarasandha, and many others when he had no practical chance.

On the criteria of the modern-day management principles of setting an objective and then achieving it by applying the management process comprising of planning, organizing, staffing, leadership, and control we would try to evaluate Shrikrishna just for the sake of the younger generations. Not that it would help him in any way but maybe some of the cobwebs in the minds of doubting Hindu people would be cleared.

Shrikrishna was a process-driven person. He would see a problem, define it, then try to find the possible solutions. Once he had decided on the solution and its process he never stopped until he accomplished the goal of solving the problem. He was intelligent enough to find a new way if the old methods were not effective. He believed in giving direct messages to the enemy as he did by beating the royal washerman in Mathura and wearing royal clothes. The sheer audacity was communicated to Kamsa, and also that Shrikrishna and Balram meant business. He killed Kamsa in full public view so that any remnant courage in the army of the Kamsa was crushed to dust. He saw to it that the throne was handed over to Ugrasen. By killing Kamsa Shrikrishna managed to announce his entry on the stage of the entire Bharatvarsha.

It is said that Sandipani Muni performed a full-fledged puja and worshipped Shrikrishna before he admitted him to his ashram as a student. He was an extraordinary student. It is said that He learned sixty-four kalas (arts) in sixty-four days. He and Balram were the top students and very popular in the ashram. Shrikrishna was so good at music that he gave lessons in veena-vaadan to Narad. Whatever he did was a lesson in perfection. He knew about horses, and he was the best sarathi of his time. He was an expert in Jyotish Shastra.

After they returned to Mathura, they had to face the wrath of Jarasandha, who was not able to accept that his mighty son-in-law was eliminated by Shrikrishna. He wanted his revenge and he tried hard. He attacked Mathura seventeen times and was defeated each time due to the excellent management of limited resources available at Mathura by Shrikrishna. Mathura was a small kingdom as compared to the Magadha and its army. But it did not matter, Jarasandha was always defeated.

When Jarasandha attacked one more time, he was helped by the Kalyavan, a yavan king. He was very powerful, and he could have damaged Mathura beyond any repairs.

The tactic used by Shrikrishna to defeat Kalyavan was a masterpiece. He played on the ego of the king. Kalyavan was a king who had a very cruel army. He attacked Mathura (the eighteenth time). Mathura was looking down the barrel and they had very a much smaller number of soldiers left. So, Shrikrishna who never wanted to harm his people for the unending cause challenged the Kalyavan to a duel. He readily agreed as he was deceived by the Manohar Swarup of the Yogeshwar. He looked so young and innocuous. So Kalyavan met Shrikrishna, in the arena. Shrikrishna after a while simply ran away. He was given a chase. While running after Shrikrishna, Kalyavan was so livid that he forgot the earlier instances where Shrikrishna had done unexpected things and got rid of his enemies. It seemed improbable, but in the end, always managed to defeat the enemy. They ran and ran. At last, Shrikrishna led Kalyavan to a cave where Muchkund king was enjoying his divine sleep after he had helped earlier the king of gods Indra to defeat the asuras in the war. He commanded the dev sena until the gods found another able commander in Karthikeya, son of Mahadeva. He was given a boon that he would sleep for years to get the rest. Anybody who wakes him up would be reduced to ashes.

Kalyavan was a son of a rishi named Shishirayan. The rishi got Kalyavan as his son was born with a boon that he would not be killed by any *shastra or Astra* and further neither by a person born in Surya or Chandra *Kul* or race, so he was practically invincible because he thought that the people from other races were incapable to defeat him. It was true to some extent, and he was very assured that he would almost be immortal. He had some connection with Jarasandha, and he was used as a master stroke by the Magadha king, as Shrikrishna was a Chandraseniya so he could not have killed the Kalyavan. The story of killing Kalyavan would not have been understood without this background. Imagine a person who needs to be eliminated and who is practically indestructible by available arms or person.

Shrikrishna was so well informed that he could manage all odds and yet get the Kalyavan eliminated. Coming back to the story,

Shrikrishna ran as if afraid of the demon, but he was the one who led the Kalyavan to the cave where Muchkund was sleeping. It was dark inside, and the visibility was low. Shrikrishna put his bright *yellow shela* or the upper cloth on the sleeping king. And Shrikrishna very cleverly hid in the dark corner of the cave. Kalyavan ran into the cave, like a raging bull, devoid of any sense. He never stopped for a moment to think about the unusual sequence of events. He was probably living in the future. He imagined life after the killing of Shrikrishna, the only thing remaining then was the *actual* killing. When he saw the yellow cloth, he just kicked the body, he was not even aware of Muchkund. Muchkund woke up like he was in a trance, when he saw Kalyavan, as per the boon of Indra, Kalyavan was reduced to ashes. He was not killed by a shastra or an Astra or by a Chandraseniya. As soon as, possible Shrikrishna put Muchkund back to his long-lost sleep. Shrikrishna returned to Mathura to the utter disgust of Jarasandha and his army.

This is a great example of a perfect execution of a plan after getting all the correct inputs to achieve the goal.

The second example is how Shrikrishna managed to kill Jarasandha in the latter years just before the Rajsuya Yadnya. Again, Jarasandha was a case of some super-human power. He was supposed to be stitched together by a Vandevi called Jara. Joined is *sandha and* Jara *is the name of the witch who joined,* hence the name, Jarasandha. He was born to two wives of the king of Magadha, but one part each. Again, a story with a fantastic angle. It is said that the father of Jarasandha was a king named, Brihadratha, who did not have a son. One sage Chandakaushika was moved by his grief and he gave the divine fruit to the king. The sage asked the king to give the fruit to his wife. The king had two wives. He loved both of them. So, he smartly divided the fruit into two halves and gave it to both queens. After the due course, they gave birth to a child but only half. The two parts were thrown into the jungle and were later joined by the Jara. The baby cried so loudly that the witch was horrified and handed over the son to the king. As a memory of the process, the kid was named Jarasandha.

Jarasandha was also the father-in-law of Kamsa. He married his two daughters, Asti, and Prapti, to the king of Mathura. After the killing of Kamsa, by Shrikrishna he attacked Mathura with twenty-three akshauhini sena (the Mahabharat war had twenty-one). Even after seventeen times he could not defeat or kill Shrikrishna, so he was smarting under the failures.

Later just before the Rajsuya Yadnya Shrikrishna decided to eliminate Jarasandha which would have made the entire Bharatvarsha sit up and take notice of the new power equations. Shrikrishna along with Bhima and Arjun went to the Magadha and challenged the king to have a duel with any one of them. Jarasandha said to Shrikrishna that he would fight Bhima as he seemed to be equal. The ensuing duel went on and on. Bhima just could not complete the duel. He was exasperated and exhausted. He looked up to Shrikrishna for advice. Shrikrishna picked up a twig, broke it, and threw the halves in opposite directions. Bhima followed the cue to the dot. He held the body of the Jarasandha. Tore him into two halves and threw the parts in two opposite directions. As the two halves could not conjoin, Jarasandha was killed.

Killing Jarasandha was for a purpose.

That he had to be killed or else he would have sided with the Kauravas in the upcoming war. Secondly, it served as a wake-up call for the kings. Moreover, Jarasandha had imprisoned eighty-four kings and wanted to sacrifice one hundred kings for some evil purpose. The liberated kings instantly came to the side of the Pandavas. One act of killing Jarasandha facilitated the Rajsuya Yadnya and because of that successful Yadnya Indraprastha was established as equal to many kingdoms.

In the auspicious premises of the Rajsuya Yadnya Shrikrishna was the main person in charge of the event management. Yet, he did many menial jobs. He looked after the arrangements. He also looked after ego management. It must have been a task. That the event was accomplished was a tribute to Shrikrishna's management skills.

One blemish if one can call so was the elimination of Shishupal, Shishupal was the cousin of Shrikrishna who was born abnormally with three eyes and four arms. His parents were about to abandon him, but there was an akashwani a divine voice that told them not to abandon him, it also said that the extra organs would disappear on the lap of a person who would be also the reason for Shishupal's death. When Shrikrishna took the newborn in his lap, the extra organs vanished. The message was clear. However, the mother of Shishupal could extract a promise from her nephew that he would not kill Shishupal until he committed one hundred sins. Out of many assignments, Shrikrishna also kept a count of the sins of his cousin. In the Yadnya mandapam, Shishupal vehemently opposed the choice of Shrikrishna for the Agra puja. Shishupal insulted Shrikrishna like never before, he insulted all kings, he even insulted Bhishma who was the proposer of Shrikrishna's name for the honour. The insult of Bhishma was the one hundred and first sin of Shishupal. When Shrikrishna declared he had enough of Shishupal's nonsense and used the powerful Sudarshan chakra to behead the erring cousin. When he saw the deadly whirring chakra Shishupal realized his death was near. He like all cowards went from person to person to save him from the wrath of the Sudarshan. He even approached Bhishma whom just a while ago he had insulted. Nobody dared to do anything and Shishupal was beheaded in full view of the supporting and opposing kings right there in the mandapam. They were simply mesmerized and stunned. The gory sight sucked whatever opposition was there and then everything went smoothly without any further problems. (Later somewhere in the seventh century a poet called Magha wrote epic poetry in Sanskrit named Shishupal-vadha, which is rated as one of the best in the top six maha kavyas in Sanskrit. It has about thousand eight hundred very well-written stanzas.)

Before the war, Shrikrishna talked to Bhishma, Karna, Shalya, and many others to plan their actions in the war. Shrikrishna believed in going all the way once the objective was decided. How else one can explain his going and asking Bhishma about how

Pandavas could kill him? He was Ajinkya (invincible) and avadhya (not to be killed) also. And he was the commander-in-chief of the Kauravas. Somehow Shrikrishna could take Draupadi to Bhishma and get a blessing 'akhanda Soubhagyavati bhav,' meaning her five husbands may live forever. Also, they would not be killed by Bhishma.

One more story where the management skills of Shrikrishna were put to the severe test was the Jayadrath killing. Jayadrath was not at all that important in the context of the war. He was one of the many who killed Abhimanyu. Arjun was out of control and vouched that he would kill Jayadrath before the sunset the next day or he would enter the blaze and finish his life.

The point to be noted is that Arjun did this stupid thing after getting the best discourse in the Geeta, just ten days ago. He was totally in control of his putramoh, and rage was caused by the loss of a son. One more thing to be noted is that Shrikrishna was not around. So, when finally, Shrikrishna came and knew about the stupid vow, he fired Arjun left-right and centre. After some time, though he became normal, he started the required planning. He instructed his sarathi Daruk to keep his chariot ready with all his shastras, in case required. There was a small matter again by way of the *boon* granted by the father of Jayadrath which complicated the task. His father Vridhakshatra had given him a boon that whoever kills Jayadrath and lets his head fall to the ground, the killer would have his head shredded into hundred pieces.

Shrikrishna knew this boon. He also knew that the old father is daily by the riverside for the evening puja. Shrikrishna was a master in astrology and hence knew that there was an eclipse that evening.

So, when the sun was covered by the shadows, the ensuing darkness was good enough for Jayadrath to appear on the scene. After all, he wanted to see the pyre of Arjun. He was not aware of what awaited him. As soon as the eclipse ended the sun came back brightly. Shrikrishna told Arjun to use pashupatastra and behead the culprit. He also told Arjun to ensure that the severed head falls into the hands of Vridhakshatra who was offering the evening prayers by the riverside. Arjun did the same, and the father and the son were eliminated.

About the management of the war, one aspect is very interesting. We tend to concentrate on the actual war, but we do not think about the support services. There is folklore about the catering activity of the war. By the time the war was about the begin every king from across India had decided whether he would be fighting for or against the Pandavas. Only one king from down south Udupi decided that he would be neutral, so he approached Shrikrishna and requested to allow the king to be the caterer. He cooked food for the entire contingent of over fifty lakhs. (Five million). He cooked every day as per the requirements, but he did not know how many would be less on the next day. The estimates were very accurate and never once the food was wasted. Upon asking how he managed, he answered very simply, he said "I do not know but I get the estimate from Shrikrishna. Every night, He likes to eat boiled peanuts. So, I give him peanuts. After some time, I take it back. If Shrikrishna has eaten twenty then the next day I cook for twenty thousand fewer people." There are some loose ends, but it gives an idea of how much they paid attention to details. Moreover, nobody knew except the two people involved.

Decision-making is one challenge all managers face. Smaller decisions are easy to make as the involved stakes are small. As the stakes grow in volume, investment, costs, expenses, control of the processes, and data handling each wrong decision can be catastrophic. We as Indians have seen many such wrong decisions and the cost we paid and still paying is running in trillions of dollars. We do not go into the details as this is not the proper forum.

The decision-making is difficult as it involves the lives of so many. Shrikrishna in his lifetime took some life-changing decisions. He has not given any obvious and specific guidelines, but we can derive some from studying his style of operations. The following steps can be useful.

1. Data collection, analysis, and application: Shrikrishna was a master in what we call today data mining and its management. In each of his achievements, he collected a great sample of data. Whether it was from the network of spies, from the visits of Narad muni, or his own astute and accurate observations, he had a fair idea about what he was up to. His intelligence department was very vast, and the communication methods were pretty complex but very fast. They used fresh horses for a distance of approximately forty miles. Either the messengers were given fresh horses, or the messengers were changed. The same person carried the replies to the earlier messages. The relays were very well managed, and they used shortcuts through hills or the shallow beds of the rivers.

He knew the importance of speedy communication.

1. Shrikrishna was very cool as they say in today's language. He was rarely excited, but he was circumspect more often. He knew that many problems have a way of sorting themselves out.
2. Decision-making: Shrikrishna was required to take decisions right from the beginning of his avatar. He had in him what we call today the prerequisites for taking sound and thorough decisions. He was extraordinarily brilliant, with a very strong imagination. He had a great analytical mind and many times he supported his decisions with very logical reasoning. His judgment was beyond compare.
3. He was always helpful to his people.
4. He was a great expert in multitasking. What he did as Shrikrishna in the avatar was improbable for one person. Simultaneously, He in his role as the **controller of the world** was working at his full capacity. Shrikrishna was in Bharatvarsha, but he had the rest of the world to control. It was so incomprehensible for some stupid pseudo-seculars that they had propagated a theory of more than one Shrikrishna. They argued about how can one person do all these mammoth tasks. After

all, they had their limited versions of greatness in their leaders who had so many faults. To imagine someone so faultless and so perfect that too in a backward nation as the Bharatvarsha was very irritating for them. Unfortunately, most of them who denigrated were Hindus.

5. Shrikrishna was a very capable person. He had so much to plan and care for and yet when it came to looking after the royal ladies imprisoned by the evil Narakasur, he accepted their responsibility in a flash. If he did not the only option available to all those ladies was to end their life. He must have spent a huge amount in providing fool-proof dignity and protection to sixteen thousand one hundred princesses. Again, the pseudo-seculars hype that he had **so many wives which is wrong**. He had eight wives and he had no intention of having a harem like the sultans. But the pseudo-seculars never talk about magnanimity. **They never question the Narakasur for imprisoning so many of them.** They never question the atrocities inflicted by their leaders on so many, for so many years, in so many countries.

Shrikrishna was a manager beyond compare. He was a solution-oriented manager. He had to face a lot of nonsense, thrust upon him by people. But he went through all the ordeals as a part of his karma.
***

CHAPTER TWELVE

What would He do now?

<u>What would He do now?</u>

As earlier mentioned, the social conditions in the Bharatvarsha in the times of Shrikrishna and the present are quite similar. The similarity is in the political, social, financial, cultural, moral, and judicial anarchy. A few of the royal family ruled and yes, they were promoted as the next to gods, and a large number called Praja suffered for no fault of theirs. People were terrified, people were in perennial doubts about whether they would live to see the next day or not. The evil people comprising of the *king, sena,* and the corrupt *Nyaya Sanstha,* were more united and enjoying all materialistic pleasures with total disregard for rules laid down by the dhramshastras. They thought that their power was absolute so much so that they declared themselves as the supreme God and forced people to abandon the rituals in the Sanatan dharma and follow the new set of rules.

The basic difference is that now the Sanatan dharma in the Bharatvarsha must fight outsiders from foreign countries and religions. They also have to fight the people who were earlier in the same Sanatan dharma but now due to various reasons do not follow the Sanatan dharma. If you look slightly deeper, they were even then not following the Sanatan dharma and due to the loose bonding with their roots, they were more gullible, they jumped to other faiths, without understanding either of them. The necessity of religion was never clear to them and it is not now. Religious conversion due to greed, hatred, force, coercion, and other factors is a questionable process and no religion allows the same. Whether they are closer to divine happiness or the promised salvation after their conversion is a matter of serious research and some of the intellectuals of both varieties (the real and pseudo) must put in some time and find out the real status of those who jumped and joined the different wagon of faith. The circumstances before the birth of Shrikrishna need to be studied. Despite the natural opulence and infinite resources, the Praja was unhappy. They were terrorized and lived in total disarray. The Praja then was *only* Hindus as the other religions were just not there. There were some tribes or sects in the Bharatvarsha who had their own set of rules, or others who were far away probably, on the other side of the globe. So, the matter was **_intra-racial,_** and not *inter-racial*, as it is today.

Was there any rulebook? Yes, there was one of the finest rulebooks. (As described in Geeta the invaluable Vedas were there.) Were the rules very rigid or difficult? No, they were quite flexible. So, the tussle was not between the followers and non-followers. The high-handedness of the rulers like the Kamsa, Jarasandha, and such kings who believed that they were better than the Gods. To make matters worse they managed to get incredible boons from gods or their parents. (Though the frequency of boons was less as compared to earlier yugas, where almost every asura was made more difficult to be eliminated by either the man or the gods. For example, Hiranyakashyapu had absolutely fantastic preconditions for protection from the gods. It was so good that a special avatar of Narsimha became necessary to kill him. Whether it was the Bhasmasur, Sund, Upsund, or Tarakasur, they did rule the world. Each story is very interesting). The kings in the Dwapar Yug were pretty close to the Kaliyuga kings as it was a sort of twilight time between the two yugas. (The death of Shrikrishna marked the beginning of the Kaliyuga.)

The point is that Praja was living in the terror. The rishis, sages, and educationists were insulted. (Just like today) Their value was questioned. The education system was twisted, exploited, and even set aside to suit the mighty. They could not pursue their studies. Pure science and research were interrupted. The power of the sword was the rule of the day. Those who were close to the ruling kings were above law. They could get away with anything like loot, rape, murder, conspiracy, bribery, and all such things. The age-old battle between the Gyan and the evil power was very much on. The *mediocrity* was dominant only because of the majority in its numbers. Intelligence, integrity, ethics, and wisdom were in short supply and whatever was available was subjected to ridicule. Again, the wise were not opposing but were patiently waiting for Shrikrishna to appear and take care of their problem and make them happy for a while until the next tyrant arrived on the scene. They would live in harmony and peace, till one more tyrant would come again, and the game would go on and on.

Does it sound familiar?

Once again, today, the Sanatan dharma is in deep trouble, so much so that the obituaries are already written. Now the problem is intra-racial, interracial, international, geographical, and also religion based. Let us see, why we Hindus face this problem, so seriously that we are facing a serious threat of being wiped off from our own country. Statistics show that we would be outnumbered by 2050 and once that happens, we would be facing a certain extinction. Just like the Parsees! But most Hindus do not want to talk about this looming danger. We have seen this kind of ethnic cleansing/ wiping off in the last one thousand years, in many countries. We have seen the aftereffect of the occupation by these oppressive forces and the practices of followers of these religions in those countries. And yet we prefer to be like an ostrich and overlook the vital matter of survival. The lame logic if *we are the oldest civilization,* or *we do not seek war* is as childish as a kid who has lost his ice cream. We are about to lose our identity as a race, and religion, and maybe our only nation which takes pride in declaring that it is not a Hindu nation.

One thing we have to remember is that there would be no more avatars and no more help from heaven. Probably, the god has also written off the *self-defeatist* Hindus. In the last century itself we lost large chunks of our nation to the ultra-religious people. We lost Burma, Lanka (Ceylon), Afghanistan, Nepal, Punjab and Sindh, and half of Bengal. As this essay is written there is a serious possibility that we may lose the entire Bengal very soon. The states of Kerala, Arunachala, Kashmir and some other areas are in a shadow of extinction. And yet we are sleeping over the issue.

The same recipe which was earlier used by the ultras to separate Kashmir from Bharat is repeated for the last seventy years. *They know what they are doing* but we do not. We are apologetic for being a Hindu, and that describes the extent of damage done to our psyche. We compromise with everything when it comes to our religion. Sadly, many in our religion are born Hindus but they claim that they are ashamed of being Hindus. They get paid or some other motivation for saying so. Nobody else does this kind of drama.

Whether our temples, our traditions, our laws, our lands, and our nation would remain with us is a big question.

If at all Shrikrishna would have to reincarnate or if he was to select someone of us to do the task of (*dharmasansthapanyarth*) re-establishment of the decaying Hindus and their minds, **what he would do**? Whether he would do anything at all or he would find it a useless exercise and leave the Hindus to fend for themselves? Hindus have to seriously think about such a possibility. Hindus do not even now realize that they have together exasperated even the most patient of gods. Like in all the three earlier Yugas, gods have helped the then-degenerating Hinduism, but the return to square one of overdependence on the gods to rectify their mistakes can be lethal for the remaining Hindus. Because once they are salvaged, they return to the <u>same evil practices</u> created in the original place, the need for divine salvation.

Or even more directly *what would you do*?

So, considering that there would be no help from the gods what would you do to re-establish, to strengthen the weakening Sanatan dharma in the Bharatvarsha?

Let us try to find out.

We have to first identify the people because of whom we are on the brink of extinction. We have to do a serious ABC analysis of who is more dangerous, and what can be done to retaliate against their actions. We have to find out why they have become strong. Who is helping them? Are they from our Bharatvarsha or they are rank outsiders? Let us see which are the major factors that are affecting the Sanatan dharma and its impending downfall. Broadly speaking they are as follows:

1. The Muslims
2. The Christians
3. The communists
4. The pseudo-seculars
5. The internal sects

We find that the above is in some way interconnected and their objective is to destroy the oldest and the wisest religion called the Sanatan dharma. All of them do not realize that they do not have anything worthwhile to replace with. Yet they say 'Let us first destroy the Sanatan dharma. Later on, we would see what to do.'

Secondly, we have to accept them as a threat.

(In the Mahabharat it is described that the control of the guru, ministry, and judiciary over the king was negligible. They were bowing in front of their practical compulsions or the perceived limits. Great characters like Dronacharya, Karna, Shakuni, and Bhishma, all succumbed to their self-imposed compulsions. The basic rule that *the rules are for the humans* and not vice versa was forgotten and they all paid a very heavy price for their misplaced judgments. All intellectuals have very dignified justifications for their errors of judgment but that does not help society. Whenever we listen to any IAS giving reasons for his failures, this fact becomes very obvious. People remember them but only as failed characters. The pseudo-intellectuals would be remembered as failures in the future.)

Presently, in India, we know the status of the administration, judiciary, and legislature, which is pathetic, to say the least. They are helped in the creation of chaos by the CAs, advocates, and petty politicians. They forget that their first allegiance is to the Bharatvarsha. The standard argument is "What can I alone do? The system is corrupt!" You can do what you can do, *do not be a part of the system*. You would earn a little less money but you would earn great self-respect which is invaluable. Moreover, all social reforms started as an individual effort.

Let us see what can be done about each threat.

1. The Muslims: Ever since the foundation of Islam in the seventh century, they are seriously trying to convert the entire world to their faith. *Nothing wrong* with it! They were moderately successful until the early nineteenth century. They have catalysed their process and in the last century, they have got Islamic power in about sixty nations. They are smart operators and conduct their operations ruthlessly. Probably converting others is one of the major unifying factors for Muslims. The concept of brotherhood is practiced very seriously.

Now the Hindus have to understand that they have to

a. Create a task force that would study Islam thoroughly. They should be able to tell the Hindus about the shortfalls in that religion. They do not have to abuse or ridicule but just report the practices. They do not have to put any views of their own or comments. They have to talk about the separate sects in Islam, separate mosques for their sects, their worshipping practices, the ridiculous laws, and so on. They should inform Hindus that they do not have to be defensive. They must also make Hindus aware of how to counter the conversion tactics. They have to raise their voice and see the difference.

b. The Christians: Many Hindus are in awe of the churches and the Mother Mary or Jesus. That can be traced back to their early education in the convents or missionary schools. Hindus should be able to differentiate between the ways of operations of the Muslims and the Christians. They are very comparable. Maybe, the Christians are slightly soft in the approach. That is all! They both want that the last standing Hindu must be converted to their faith. NOTHING wrong with it. They are brought up like that. They believe in the spread of religion in any which way possible,

Again, it is advised we should have some dedicated intellectuals to study Christianity. They must find out the anomalies in their religion. If every Christian is the same in front of God, why separate churches, why so many sects? Why so much mystery around Good Friday and easter?

Again, in the words of J. Krishnamurthy, it becomes very clear. "*IN A LARGE enclosure, among many trees, was a church. People, brown and white, were going in. Inside there was more light than in the European churches, but the arrangements were the same. The ceremony was in progress and there was a beauty. When it was over, very few of the brown talked to the white or the white to the brown, and we all went our different ways.*" It is clear that even if you are a Christian your acceptance as a human being is not certain.

"*On another continent, there was a temple, and they were singing a Sanskrit chant; the Puja, a Hindu ceremony, was being performed. The congregation was of another cultural pattern. The tonality of Sanskrit words is very penetrating and powerful; it has a strange weight and depth.*"

So, the Hindus have to be assertive without being aggressive, ready for a tit-for-tat type of argument but always assume a higher plane. Hindus have to understand that despite all the perceived and programmed shortcomings, Sanatan dharma is much better than any other existing way of life. So, instead of being defensive, they must be pleasantly assertive. From the life of Swami Vivekananda, we can learn how many times he pleasantly retaliated against the presumptuous attacks of the Sanatan dharma and won the arguments without actually starting one. There are many others like Aurobindo, Swami Chinmaynanda, J. Krishnamurthy, and the new generation Jaggi Vasudev who can teach the practical ways of tackling objections. The argument about our Sanatan dharma with any other religion with no logical base *is useless*. The moment you compare to give them a status of being at least worth argument which they are not. The best way is to let them prove that they are worth it. Instead of convincing a nonbeliever he should spend that time in the development of his understanding and use that for the betterment of fellow Hindus.

1. The Christians: What most of us forget when we refer to Christianity is that it originated in the very vicinity of Islam and Judaism. It is a small area in the middle east where these religions along with the monotheist faith. Christ was a born Jew and later he became the founder of Christianity. There are many grey areas in the two religions that we as an affected party must know and use as an argument. There are many interactions in all three religions and they have common names, places, and shared sacred places in these religions. Constantinople, today's Istanbul was and is the major center for the activity of these religions. We have seen many times in the past that there is an inherent soft corner for each other and more often than not the Muslims and Christians have united against the Hindus.

Nothing of the above would have mattered to the Sanatan dharma had they not spoilt the Hindu way of life. The Sanatan dharma had survived, prospered, and was spreading the message of Shrikrishna all over the world. There was no coercion, and also no barbarism involved. When they both invaded Bharat and they looted, cheated, spoilt the worship places, converted Hindus by force, created false impressions, and generally told the Hindus that they are an inferior race. The sad part is some stupid Hindus believed and started licking their boots.

Presently, in the Hindu context when they deal with Christians they are confused as many converts are still with their old Hindu names. They use their Hindu names as and when convenient for them. The churches are not under the control of the government and huge properties at the prime locations are with the churches. Like all around the world, these religious places are used for nefarious activities though nothing can be *proved legally*. They support anti-India activities. Again, covertly. You may talk to any person in the church and they would speak very decent ways, but they would indicate that their way of life is better than the Sanatan dharma. These organizations can be very dangerous to the survival of the Sanatan dharma as they are hand in hand with the Vatican, NGOs, and very rich foundations. Hindus must keep a track record and try to defend their religion. If we have to put ratings based on the dangers, that can cause to the Sanatan, dharma, we can say that Islam is more dangerous, but at the same time, we should never forget that the Christians are not very far behind. *For us they both are bad.* None of them loves our country. They see Bharat as a colony that needs to be exploited. When the time of final choice would arrive, they would most likely select their foreign masters. That is what appears at least as of today. Christians have used the Congress government in a very smooth way to increase their numbers in the northeast and Central India. We do not know who is with us so as Shrikrishna would tell us we should consider both of them as adversaries. We must fight them on all fronts. Either they fall in our line or be a dedicated enemy.

3. The Communists: The Communists in India are one of the smartest operators. When nowhere in the world communism is alive, India has one state ruled by them. In its entire history since its inception, they have nothing great achieved. They destroyed our freedom struggle, our history, our culture, our education, our industries, and our development plans, and yet they have shamelessly tried to demean the Bharatvarsha. They openly supported China, in the 1962 war. They have compromised their

negligible sense of dignity with the party every time the nation wanted them not to. They have nothing to show as their accomplishments in their total tenure of existence. Of course, they can show the ruins of JNU, West Bengal, the closure of the textile industry, the steel industry, the coal sector, the delays in the construction of dams, and the lopsided labour movements where **only rights** of the labour are discussed but never talk about the responsibility of the labour. Maximum loss to Indian development is because of these pseudo-intellectuals who are paid pets of foreign countries. These people always talk about stupid baseless things. Every time the government gave them a chance to run the industry which they had forced into lockdown, they failed miserably. They could not because they have never done anything worthwhile in their lives. Over one hundred years of active existence with nothing showing on the credit side is the real balance sheet of the communist party. Yes, they have created cancer called Naxalism in the states of Bihar, Bengal, Chhattisgarh, Maharashtra, and Andhra Pradesh. Also, they have reduced their movement into a criminal association involved in extortion, kidnapping, and terrorism. The earlier version based on the ideology of Sanyal and Majumdar is dead long ago.

Communism is reduced to hyper-parasitism in India, but it can cause damage. They must be silenced forever. Even Muslims can be a better choice than the communists.

The communists have started a new trend of urban Naxalism through which they give cover fire to the terrorists, and the poisonous student leaders and they use the concept for maligning the image of Bharatvarsha. In their global existence, the communists cannot show one place or process, as their success. They have failed on all accounts, so as last resort they are concentrating all their evil energies to cause maximum damage to India.

We must fight them as brutally as possible, sometimes even more forcefully than the other two. They are the worst.

4. The pseudo-seculars: This is a relatively new race in India. It started as a section of the then Bhartiya society who were bending their backs to prove that they are not the Sanatan. They had first learned Farsi, Urdu, and then English just to please their new masters. They were the first anti-Sanatan gang who had to grind their axe by denigrating Hinduism and Vedic traditions. Because they had support from very willing rulers, they could influence the course of history in a great way. They had a loud voice which amplified the wrong messages and more likely the messages the rulers wanted. They worked overtime to find out the *faults* in the system. Sadly, they never had anything better to replace the faults. In the case of sati-pratha however, they corrected a major fault. But that was one of the very few exceptions. In each state of India, they were in different groups. They had some special privileges granted by the rulers. Sadly, they never realized the greatest damage they were causing to their motherland which had survived very nicely without the so-called forward social customs. But as we know the saying in Sanskrit 'sarve guna kanchanam ashryante' means the rich and powerful automatically get all qualities.

Now in modern India, the pseudo-seculars are much more advanced than their ancestors. They have perfected systems and they use the AV media to the hilt. Many names have brought shame to broadcasting, anchoring, media interviews, panel discussions, and yellow reporting. They are the worst in the case of abusing Hinduism. We must treat these people who have a hidden agenda as dedicated enemies. Their properties must be attached, they should be boycotted, their activities must be opposed at each stage, and anybody who supports them should be boycotted. The Hindus have to unite against this kind of garbage and deal with them on a case-to-case basis. The Hindus must remember that whether they fight or not, whether they submit to the utter nonsense of the pseudo-seculars, whether they accept or oppose they would be taken to a stage where they would have to *physically fight* all of the above anti-

Hindu factions in the Bharatvarsha. The pseudo-seculars would see to it that the Hindus are taken to a stage where they would either have to fight or perish.

5. The internal sects: The people who are anti-Hindus, tell us that one of the major shortfalls in Hinduism is the caste and sect system. They also tell as if no other religion has such divisions. They ridicule the Hindus and their system of division based on karma. They try to assume a position of a higher plane and shamelessly keep on repeating unnecessary information to us. What they forget is the Sanatan dharma does not need any external nonsense. What should the Hindus know about the division of mankind around the world is much worse than the Hindu way of society. Christians have their dirty divisions, so also the Muslims. The Sanatan dharma followers must know that there are about seventy-two sects in Islam and about three hundred further divisions. None of them considers other sects as Muslims and kills each other as a routine. The rift between the Shia and Sunni is famous but there are many others. They have separate worship places, where nobody else is allowed. In the brotherhood concept, the black Muslims, the Indian Muslims, the Wahabis, and so many others are fighting each other, but they have the gumption to tell the Hindus about the caste system.

The Christians have Catholics, and Orthodox Protestants, as the main divisions. They have separate controls; separate churches and may be variations in the holy books. Apart from these, there are many unsaid divisions. There is a colour, regional, and many others divisions but they are never talked about. What the outsiders know is the properly dished-out content. The Hindus do not know much about Islam or Christianity and he is not bothered much. This is in line with his thinking as he hardly knows anything about Hinduism. So, when he is ignorant of his own religion and faith he cannot be expected to know about other religions. This situation has to change, Hindus must know about all religions, in detail which would help them to fight the stupid allegations. The knowledge about the Sanatan dharma would enhance his self-esteem which would prove to be the only fuel to fight the impending onslaught on him his religion and his region shortly. Fighting unnecessarily and fighting for the survival of his religion his way of life is altogether different.

The Hindus must understand that unless human society is divided or *to use a better word* classified it cannot have an order. As time progresses new classifications emerge. For example, today a new class of people is emerging

a) those who know how to use computers,

b) program them,

c) produce hardware,

d) aware of AI,

e) cloud computing,

f) and many such things only in computers.

Earlier it was classified based on knowledge of Sanskrit, then Farsi, English, and nothing much has changed except for the item of division.

In India, we specialize in dividing. We create new divisions and we keep on fighting. For example

- On a regional basis: (east-west/north-south/coastal- mainland/ hilly area –plains/ and so many others
- Religion basis: Hindu, Muslim, Christian, Sikh, Jain, Buddhist, Parsees, and Jews. Further, there must be many more internal divisions of each of the above.
- Language basis: each language creates a division and now the dialects also follow the trend.
- Status as per the statute.

The Hindus never seem to learn from their blunders in the last two thousand years.

Whatever our conditions we should never accept that others are better as in fact they are not. We do not go and prove it but assert that we are the best.

***

When we have to find out what we have to do to correct the situation we have to first find out what was done wrong. A mentally strong race, which could rule the world without ever invading any country suddenly finds itself on the brink of disaster. What worked for the Hindus before the invasion of Islam could not survive the barbaric and cruel attacks on Bharat. There was a cultural shock as the Hindus did not believe in massacring the people, especially males when they won any war. Most likely the eldest son would be made the king and a hefty sum towards the expenses and taxes would be recovered. But the land was not annexed. Similar logic continued even when Ashok ruled India. When Prithviraj Chauhan was defeated by Muhammad Ghori, with the help of Jaichand, he was brutalized beyond limits. That he killed the sultan etc became folklore but that embarked on the darkest chapter in the history of Bharat. The darkest chapter continued till 1947, with the change of the oppressors, Turks, Moghuls, Portuguese, French, and British.

In 1947, the country was divided into three illogical parts, two were dedicated Islamic states and one was without any religion and any sense, that one mistake is bleeding heavily and may lead to the loss of our nation if we do not do something drastic. Presently it is like one man running a race and the other taking a leisurely stroll without a worry. The one who is running is already way ahead in terms of the preparations to make this country into an Islamic nation. The others like Christians are doing the same things as the Muslims but they are slightly more subtle. Again, the Hindus who are sleeping both physically and figuratively would most likely wake up when it would be very late. The Hindus so far have not understood the game of numbers. In 1900 there were very fewer Christians in India, but due to constant patronage of both the British and Congress rule, many states have increased numbers of Christians. Similarly, the Muslim count is increasing by four times than what was in 1947. Add to it the reduced number of Hindus in the neighbouring countries from approximately 20 percent to 2 percent and one would understand the severity of the problem. Everybody else would but not the Hindus! And if the Hindus belong to the pseudo-secular types, then they would pick up fights with the facts. Even today any tinpot minority leaders can get away with saying anything defamatory about the Hindus. There is no concerted opposition, there is no unity, and hence no nuisance value. Hindus still consider Muslims as the minority when they would be a miserable minority very soon. By definition of minority has to be less than five percent of the population but it is not so. Moreover, in the states where the minorities are in majority, the Hindus are not treated as minorities, like in J and K or Nagaland. Even in some districts in UP, Bihar, Bengal, Maharashtra, Kerala, and Haryana the Hindus are living a miserable life. In any area where there is more percentage of Muslims, we get a feeling of entering Pakistan. And that can be verified. Again, the Muslims or the Christians cannot be blamed. The only people who are to be blamed would be the Hindus, who cannot dominate their own nation.

If the Hindus cannot fight for their religion, their own families, and their own culture then they deserve to perish. They do not have to hate anyone, but they have to at least love their own. They have to care for their own. They do not have to be apologetic for being a Hindu at least in the Hindustan.

Why the Hindus are easy targets for religious conversion? The first, of the reasons that surfaces, is the loose control of the Sanatan dharma over its followers. Sanatan dharma expects a person following it to be a mature one. A big mistake, in the present context. There are quite a few confusions in the minds of the remaining Hindus, and they are allowed to express them. They can question, can ridicule their value systems. But very few realize that these questions are planted in their minds by the people who wanted the decline of the Sanatan dharma. The ones who were converted never really knew their dharma and they never know their new one. Moreover, they cannot question it as it amounts to blasphemy, punishable severely.

When the towns, areas, and provinces were converted to Islam the Hindus, never bothered. Now it hurts. The return to Sanatan dharma must be facilitated. There must be a campaign to re-admit those gullible Hindus who were converted by fraud. He would devise a system to welcome back the ones who want to return to the sanity of Sanatan dharma.

The Hindus have a treasure lying idle, but we cannot read it in the original language. He would revive Sanskrit in a phased manner. Sanskrit is the real binder, not English or Hindi.

History teaches us the right things if it is documented correctly. We cannot say so about our own. We have a vacuum of thousands of years in the time scale. History was wiped off by many. He would rewrite history and make the Hindus realize that they have everything to be proud of. The dispassionate account with facts, without any nonsense of secularism, would be much better than the present trash that is thrust down the throats of the Hindu kids.

He would re-establish the temple systems. The forefathers were not constructing temples just for the sake of worshipping. Each temple is constructed to maximize positive energy. The feeling of Jagrut Dev comes from this unique construction design. The feeling of somebody being there is due to the similarity of the body and the temple. The inner Sanctorum of both is very significant and revered. He would tell us that each temple is a healthy system in itself. The temple concept would be revitalized and the social engineering to create a bond between the society would be created, using the temples. Sadly, the management of only Hindu temples is under the government. The revenue generated here is misused by successive governments and even more sadly used against Hindu interests. He would fight for the rights of the management of Hindu establishments. Or all the establishments of all religions must be *nationalized*. It would not be easy, but we must fight for it like our life depends on it. He would reorganize the management of temples. The Christians and the Muslims have perfected the system of temples and successfully exploited the same. The latest to join the temple scheme are the Sikhs through their Gurudwaras and the neo-Buddhists through their Viharas. There is nothing original in the concept of the temples, but it seems that they are using it better than the Hindus.

There is one more major stupidity going around on purpose. That is blaming Hindus for being communal. He would *redefine* the concept of communalism if it were worthwhile, or just plainly scrap it. Sanatan dharma does not need lectures on this useless topic. The least by the communists who have neither back nor front or the backbone.

He would teach the Hindus to stop being naïve. He would tell that unity with Muslims or Christians is a myth. If it is still alive in many ways, it is at the expense of the Hindus. The religions which believe in forceful and fraudulent conversions would never allow them when they are more in numbers. So, we have to be forceful in our interests.

He would teach us not to be apologetic, for being a Hindu. Whether by will or against their will the Hindus are responsible for a major part of the wealth in the world. The core of most religions comes from the Sanatan dharma. Again, very debatable!

He would teach us to live with our heads held high, and compete with the best in the world. He would teach us to be emotional and brave. He would teach us to practice non-violence only if helps our cause. He would teach us that for anything to help us we have to be alive.

He would teach us to be aware of the timeline. He would tell us that we have very few decades to get back our prestige and pride. He would teach us to unite and fight for our causes. He would tell us that nobody else would do it for us.

He would tell us to create a fear of what Hindus can do. He would tell us to increase our nuisance value. He would teach us to retaliate. He would teach us to live in peace only of it is beneficial to us. Peace at the cost of our land, our religion, our culture, our future, and our lives, is useless.

Finally, he would teach us to be self-reliant. To have faith in him that he would help us only when he finds that we have put in our best effort and then we still need some push here and a prod there.

Start doing something for the betterment of the Sanatan dharma, and he would help. Or else we would not need anything.

So, unite, rise, and fight for the Sanatan dharma, which is the most beautiful thing in the world.

***

Epilogue.

<u>Epilogue.</u>

Shrikrishna is someone beyond creation, comparison, comprehension, and even any calculation. <u>We see him as we see him, not *what* he is</u>! We feel he is sweet, he is full of mischief, full of joy so we like him. Yes, he is like that, but he is much more than that. We are not very inclined to see his philosophy, as many times it shows us the mirror through which we avoid looking in. When we graduate from seeing his adorable form of childhood to his Gyani form, we are slightly uncomfortable, and we want to shift as soon as possible to his Manohar Roopam.

We are not alone.

Even when Arjun was listening to Geeta, inside he was finding it incredible that his one-time friend is deciphering the complex codes of life in such a great but simple way. Somehow, Shrikrishna realized that he would have to authenticate his credentials as the only *ONE* who alone matters, alone who creates and destroys, alone who controls, then he decided to show his *virat*/-gigantic-/ Swarup to his friend, who had lost his will to fight. There is a thought that Shrikrishna was not formally attached even to Arjun, but he had earlier decided that Arjun would be the formal symbol- the *nimitta matra*- for the intended destruction of unworthy people. There was no more time to waste, and he had no alternative if Arjun was incapacitated to fight. The whole careful planning of decades would have been rendered useless. Shrikrishna could not have afforded the same to happen. So, he blessed Arjun with the divine vision- the Divya Drishti- and displayed the real Him, in His Vishwaroopdarshan. Shrikrishna told Arjun to see what he could see, to understand what he could, which Arjun was not ready for. Despite the Divya Drishti and all, Arjun could not see the entire Virat Swarup. Whatever little he could see was beyond his understanding and it was in contrast to a person who was so mild and friendly. The entire universe that too in its operative mode, not like a photograph but like a motion picture, in one manifestation of a single form, is simply unimaginable, and hence it is the Shrikrishna we do not seem to know. What Arjun saw we cannot know, but it says in Geeta that he saw things that were beyond his *extraordinary* comprehension. He saw that the people whom he was supposed to kill in the future were already being destroyed, he saw that the Ananta, *amurta (intangible)*, with innumerable mouths, wearing the clothes he had never seen before, with the weapons and astras, with the creation and destruction on the same form. He could not fathom the beginning or see the end of it, he was stunned, and then finally he understood a little bit of the Shrikrishna and surrendered in full humility and prayed to Him to return to his normal adorable form. Arjun promised that he would fight and no more he would be confused about what he should do. He would follow the instructions in implicit faith and trust and would not worry about the results.

Just imagine that the whole episode of Shrikrishna telling the Geeta right in the middle of Kurukshetra, to a totally crestfallen, confused, nearly amorphous form of Arjun and also imagine the after effect of the revitalized and revamped Arjun into one of the best fighting machines and then you would probably realize the power of the great Shrikrishna. He was not ready to deliver, there was no prior indication, no prior preparation, he delivered one of the most complicated messages in very concise, clear, colourful, and compulsive narration in an extempore way. He composed all those seven hundred shlokas on the site describing the secrets of life, fights, salvation, why to do and what to do, to do without expecting anything in return, and so many other things just like that. What he said that day on the battlefield is still being decoded by the most brilliant brains and every day some new meanings are found. If Shrikrishna was to deliver only the Geeta, he would have been remembered eternally. The Geeta formed a fraction of his entire being, tells us about the incomprehensible and incalculable character of Shrikrishna.

Shrikrishna is a Purnavtar and he is the closest to human beings as the god who moved with the humans. Maybe because he was so easily available to the humans, they did not appraise his full potential. He can be studied in four basic forms. As a visionary, strategist, complete avatar, and as philosopher.

Shrikrishna is once in a *yug- /age/ -* phenomenon and hence he is rightly called a yugpurush. That he was a complete Purusha or a Purushottam (best in the entire purushas) at that, is beyond any debate. No other words like a legend or an icon can describe the phenomenon of Shrikrishna. What he achieved in each part of his life is in itself much more than many have in many births. No character in the entire known and unknown history of human beings comes anywhere near the completeness of the great Shrikrishna. He led his life with complete control and authority. He was clear about the purpose of his life and how to accomplish the same.

He could have accomplished all he wanted to in a fraction of a second, but he chose a long and circuitous way of getting the job done by others. When he selected his personnel, he spent a lot of time teaching and training them to do what he wanted them to do. When one reads the Bhagwat, the Mahabharata, it becomes clear that in the entire period of one hundred and twenty-five years of his life, the only person who knew what was happening was the one and only Shrikrishna. All others had a partial view and even that was much more than they could handle. They were all a part of a mega plot that had only one director, Shrikrishna., The others could never know what they were doing, why they were doing it, and what would be the results. There were a few like Vidur, Bhishma, and Vyas who were aware of the extraordinary, complete, and divine nature of Shrikrishna, but they also could not move out of the script and change it. They just followed their roles and except for Vyas, at last, met their logical end.

The greatest amusing part of the character of Shrikrishna is the patience he had in sustaining the time spent, the various mistakes, and the usual and unusual family tussles by the people around him.

He was a part of a magnum opus, himself, and he played it to perfection whether it was the case of accepting Gandhari's illogical curse, or the recovery of the Syamantak gem (which was creating twenty bhars of gold every day), the great *alumni* meet if we can call it so, with Sudama, the beheading of Shishupal, the efficient management in the Rajsuya Yadnya, the unique way in which he helped Draupadi when she had no one else, the skillful handling of the negotiations before the war, the ruthless and focussed way in which he handled the complete operations of the war, the donning of the chakra and attacking the great Bhishma, the killing of Jayadrath was incomparable. He could have done just any one of these and still, he would be remembered as the greatest man who ever lived.

About thirty years after the war, it is said that he was approached by the Brahmadev and was reminded that time is fast approaching for the end of the avatar. Shrikrishna said, yes, he could go back to Vaikuntha, but for the unruly Yadavas. He explained that the Yadavas had become so powerful that they could be a very plausible reason for yet another avatar. He said that he could not leave the elimination to anyone else. He would himself see to it that the unruly, mighty, unbridled Yadavas meet their logical end before they end his avatar. The Yadavas could have defeated anyone and everyone. They were made invincible by their association with Shrikrishna. Many of them were very hot-tempered and powerful. So, he had to plan an *implosion-like* strategy that would ensure the self-destruction of the Yadavas. It was the only way where the rest of the world would be unaffected. Shrikrishna did not want to leave anything that the lesser mortals could not handle in the later era. He could have avoided the annihilation of his clan, after all, he was the one who revived a stillborn child of the Uttara. He had accomplished so much, and he could have easily at least deferred the destruction, but he decided to go ahead and that would be his last avatar Karya. What parameters he applied before finally deciding that the time for the *vinash had arrived,* would never be known to us, but the mistakes, arrogance, blasphemy, and fall in morality and ethics of the Yadavas must have helped Shrikrishna to a large extent. Once he decided, he moved at his usual speed and accomplished the task with clinical precision.

The *mousal Parva* in the Mahabharat is one of the most disturbing chapters of his life. It describes the total destruction of a very powerful dynasty called the Yadavas. Whether they were from the Vrushni or the Andhak clans, they shared one basic character they were all becoming just like the people like Kamsa or Jarasandha. They forgot the restrictions and the discipline of their illustrious heritage. So, Shrikrishna took them to Prabhas Tirthkshetra and waited for the inevitable. As expected, the Yadavas paid no heed to the rules to be followed at any holy place. They all drank wine and were soon out of control. Some arguments were nasty. In one such argument, Satyaki beheaded Kritvarma, and then the mayhem started. Within a few hours, the mighty Yadavas were nullified in the incident now referred to as the Yadavi, meaning the fierce infighting. Shrikrishna saw to it that no one survived, not even his own sons. (So, the present-day Yadavas claiming the lineage of Shrikrishna must prove their claim.) The only survivor was the great Uddahv who had proceeded to the Badrikashram for his penance.

All those, who are his followers need to understand a basic thing. That he succeeded more because of his planning and not because he was divine. **There were plans to kill him even before he was born.** The efforts to finish him continued, till finally, he killed his uncle, the evil Kamsa. He faced the problems and his enemies either head-on as per the demand of the situation. He continued to fight with whatever resources he had. At times he even fled from the scene. But he never fell prey to the temptation of self-pity or shortcuts. He never resorted to the mantra tantra processes. He never checked his horoscope. Neither he undertook pilgrimages nor depended on the holy men. He believed in the concept of Karma and he promoted the same throughout his lifetime. He gave a full session (*Bhagwat Geeta*) on the way to success in the middle of the battlefield to Arjun. He never checked his horoscope of Arjun.

But he literally **reformed** him in a matter of short time. He warned Arjun that no one else would fight the war for Arjun. At the same time, he promised Arjun that he would use all his resources to see that Arjun would become a winner. That Shrikrishna was a driver (Sarathi) of the chariot for Arjun was not only in physical form but extended to the metaphysical form. Shrikrishna not only charted the course of the chariot but also the lives of the Pandavas. The message is clear. He would help only those who want to follow the path of Karma.

Once he had finished his avatarkarya Shrikrishna proceeded to Vaikuntha succumbing to the injury to the heal by an arrow shot by an ordinary hunter named Jara. When he saw what his arrow had done, he was aghast. Shrikrishna gave him the final advice. The hunter was the last person he talked to. For a very dramatic life, his death was really an anti-climax type, but then that was Shrikrishna in his best mystical ways.

***

www.ingramcontent.com/pod-product-compliance
Lightning Source LLC
Chambersburg PA
CBHW060921140726
47996CB00001B/332